In Search of the Common Good

Guideposts for Concerned Citizens

In Search of the Common Good

Guideposts for Concerned Citizens

Jack E. Brush

BOOKS

Winchester, UK
Washington, USA

First published by iff Books, 2016

iff Books is an imprint of John Hunt Publishing Ltd., Laurel House, Station Approach,
Alresford, Hants, SO24 9JH, UK
office1@jhpbooks.net
www.johnhuntpublishing.com
www.iff-books.com

For distributor details and how to order please visit the 'Ordering' section on our website.

Text copyright: Jack E. Brush 2014

ISBN: 978 1 78535 291 1
Library of Congress Control Number: 2015956002

A CIP catalogue record for this book is available from the British Library.

Design: Lee Nash

Printed in the USA by Edwards Brothers Malloy

CONTENTS

Preface

With regard to its subject matter and underlying concern, the present work is a sequel to my book entitled *Citizens of the Broken Compass: Ethical and Religious Disorientation in the Age of Technology* (2015), but it differs from the latter in its context and structure. Whereas *Citizens of the Broken Compass* was a series of ten more or less independent essays that originated as talks in various clubs, *In Search of the Common Good* was conceived from the outset as a literary work with a systematic structure. To the extent possible, technical distinctions have been avoided and foreign language expressions have been translated. As the title indicates, the work is not addressed to an academic group of specialists, but rather to a general readership, i.e. to concerned citizens who are interested in thinking through some of the ethical and moral issues facing us today. Since footnotes have been held to a minimum, the informed reader will recognize that my indebtedness to other authors goes far beyond the credits given.

I would like to thank my friend Alan S. Gold, United States District Court Judge for his helpful comments about Chapter 7 in which several Supreme Court cases are mentioned. Should my presentation of the legal aspects of a particular case seem inadequate to the specialist, I would like to point out that my major interest in this book is ethical-philosophical rather than legal and that I have introduced legal cases only as illustrations of complicated moral issues.

Finally, my heartfelt thanks go once again to my wife Susan L. Brush without whose support and assistance the writing of this essay would not have been possible. Not only her patience during the hours that I spend at my desk, but also her willingness to discuss central issues with me in our leisure time are invaluable.

Jack Edmund Brush

Introduction

In *Citizens of the Broken Compass*, I alluded to a work by Charles Dickens entitled *The Lazy Tour of Two Idle Apprentices* in which he writes: "The compass is broken, and the exploring party is lost!" The metaphor of the "broken compass" describes well the cultural situation in which we find ourselves today. The technological achievements of the last centuries are an astonishing testimony to the rational capacity of human beings, but the discrepancy between our technological ability and our ethical and moral sensitivities is not only obvious, but deeply disturbing. We know *how* to do many things, but we have difficulty deciding whether such things *should* be done. It is relatively easy for the scientist to claim neutrality on many controversial issues by pointing out that science deals with that which *is* the case, not with that which *ought* to be the case. That is, science is concerned with facts, not values. But given the situation of the world today—the danger of nuclear war, the threat of climate disaster and so forth—, the claim of neutrality by anyone, be it a scientist, an attorney or a musician, is unacceptable in any society. Every citizen of the world community is called upon today to address crucial moral and ethical issues, and this call is all the more demanding on those who are privileged with the means to make significant changes.

As mentioned in the Preface, the present work *In Search of the Common Good* is a continuation of the issues addressed more informally in *Citizens of the Broken Compass*. Whereas the latter was a collection of talks held in various clubs, the former is an extended essay on the problem of balancing human rights and the common good. Strictly speaking, I would not characterize this essay as a work on ethics or even on morality. Rather than presenting certain moral standards or a systematic ethics, *In Search of the Common Good* discusses three guideposts that may be helpful in making moral and political decisions. Admittedly, guideposts do not guarantee safe passage along a pathway, but when the exploring party is lost and the compass is broken, guideposts may be a welcome sight. The purpose of the guideposts is not to replace the concept of human rights, but rather to provide a context of interpretation. Any attempt to replace human rights in our world would undoubtedly be catastrophic since rights are the only shred of moral standard that we still possess. That notwithstanding, rights have proven to be an inadequate standard, and they must, therefore, be supplemented and contextualized.

In order to arrive at the desired guideposts for interpreting human rights, we will have occasion to investigate two concepts that were very closely related in the Hellenistic philosophy of the first century BC: natural law and natural right. Both of these concepts have survived in modern times, albeit in a considerably different form. Out of the ancient concept of natural law, scientists have developed the idea of the laws of nature (Chapter 2), and out of the concept of natural right, political philosophers and ethicists have developed the modern notion of human rights (Chapter 6). The process in which these changes occurred extended over several centuries and has resulted in an ethical relativism that still plagues us today. In Chapter 3, we will suggest how this relativism could be overcome. In Chapters 4 and 5, we will sketch out a new understanding of natural law, taking as our starting point the modern concept of the self, and in Chapter 6, we will broaden our perspective to include the notion of the common good. In the final chapter, we will describe the moral guideposts that we consider essential as a context of the interpretation for human rights—guideposts that will hopefully promote the common good.

Chapter 1

The Eclipse of Power
and Loss of Moral Authority

No impartial observer can fail to recognize the similarities between the underlying mentalities of the extreme, right-wing, militant groups that have developed within the three world religions which trace their heritage back to Abraham: Judaism, Christianity and Islam. To be sure, none of these three religions should be described categorically as militant. Nevertheless, each of them does contain a militant element which exhibits a fanatical intolerance for others, an inability to carry on meaningful dialogue, an almost sadistic inclination to the destruction of life and property, and above all a glorification of violence. One often speaks of the radicalism of such movements, but on purely linguistic grounds, the designation "radical" seems inappropriate. The word "radical" is a Latin derivative and has the basic meaning of "being rooted" in something. In my opinion, the above mentioned movements do not deserve this designation precisely for the reason that they are not rooted at all. The violence that they perpetrate is not the result of their being rooted deeply in their own cultures, in their own religious traditions or in anything else; their unleased violence has no roots at all and therefore no limits and no boundaries. Violence has become a way of trying to establish their identity — an identity that has been hopelessly lost. In a healthy society, the identity of individuals and of groups is established through participation in various institutions of the culture such as political parties, professional organizations and religious groups. In particular, religion has always played a pivotal role in this regard. However, when religion in its true form no longer provides grounding for the individual, when it no longer helps

1

the individual establish his or her self-understanding and self-identity, that is to say, when religion loses its contact with the divine, then the empty forms of religion become susceptible to the darker side of human nature and often develop into aggressive, hostile, violent movements. How this has happened in Judaism, Christianity and Islam is a historically complex matter, and in this chapter we will consider only Christianity in its Western form.

In order to understand violent movements, we must distinguish first of all between power, force and violence. In the political-societal realm, *power* is quite distinct from *force*. Whereas force compels and coerces, power persuades and convinces. Whereas the physical world is the medium of force, language is the medium of power. We speak of moving heavy objects by sheer force, whereby the force may be produced directly by the exertion of human muscles or by machines designed by humans. In either case, the force is applied according to the laws of physics, and the objects are moved from one place to another. If similar forces are applied to human "objects", then they too can be compelled to move in this or that direction. In general, we can coerce other human beings to obey our will either by the threat or by the actual exercise of force. The intensity of the force can range from a slap in the face to the explosion of an atomic bomb, but the principle remains the same. We coerce others to obey our will by the use of force. When such force becomes destructive of life and property, as in the case of warfare, then the boundary has been crossed from force to *violence*. Through violence, we not only coerce others, we destroy them. In contrast to both force and violence, *power* has the uncanny quality of changing people's hearts and minds without the use of coercion. A dramatic speech can have tremendous power. Properly conducted diplomacy can have a powerful impact. Although language is the medium of power, the power need not be verbally expressed at every moment in time; we also speak of the moral authority of an

2

individual or a group, und such authority can be extremely powerful.

Even during the cultural revolution of the 1960s, there were still signs of real power in American society. There was still some sense of moral authority in domestic as well as foreign affairs, and there were orators like Martin Luther King, Jr. who truly moved people with the power of their words. Today, there are far fewer signs of such power. The moral authority of the United States has suffered greatly, and powerful speeches have been replaced to a large extent by sound bites and advertising gimmicks. In the public mind, *force* is now understood as an expression of great power. It is generally thought that "powerful" nations exert their force on other nations and control their destinies, and as a "superpower", the United States extends its armed "forces" across the globe, perpetrating violence in order to attain its ends.

Contrary to public opinion, however, true power does not require the threat or the actual use of force and violence. In fact, where violence becomes the standard of the day, true power has disappeared from the scene. In her book *On Violence* (1970), Hannah Arendt analyses the concepts of power, force and violence, and she comes to the following conclusion: Power and violence are inversely proportional to each other. Where there is real power, violence is not necessary. Where violence is perpetrated daily, power has ceased to exist. Given these definitions, it would be more appropriate to say that the United States has become a super-force, rather than a super-power. It was the first nation to develop a nuclear weapon, the only nation to ever use a nuclear weapon in warfare, and is today the undisputed super-force in the world, capable of massive acts of violence through a simple mouse click. But in many ways, the United States is still struggling to understand true power, and Hollywood has not been much help in the endeavor. One need only think of popular films that glorify the ability of the military to destroy through acts of violence. Yet, one cannot lay the entire blame for the present state of affairs on the shoulders of Hollywood producers. The reasons for the eclipse of power in our time and the concomitant outbreak of violence on all sides are far more complex than Hollywood producers could imagine. In part, this development is due to the lack of existential meaning in Western societies and the emptiness of traditional religious forms, which we mentioned above. It is no accident that these empty religious forms are now being filled with new content in order to justify violence. The rationale goes something like this: we are not really slaughtering other human beings, we are saving the civilized world from savages, just as "God" has commanded us to do. Yet, this abuse of religion would never have been possible, if other factors had not contributed to the eclipse of power.

In my volume on faith in the age of science (*Glauben als Ereignis: Selbst, Kraft, Zeit, Leben*, 2011), there is an extended discussion concerning the development of natural science in the seventeenth and eighteenth centuries that demonstrates how the new scientific concept of force eclipsed the older and more fundamental concept of power.[1(p159–182)] We see the beginnings of a new concept of force in the writings of Johannes Kepler, but it was in the work of Sir Isaac Newton that the notion of force really began to replace power. In what became known as the "Newtonian World Machine", the entire universe was thought to be moved by physical forces. Since everything that took place in this mechanical world was caused by some physical force, even God's interaction with the world was conceived in this manner. Whereas the theological tradition had always spoken of God's omnipotence, meaning God's attribute of being all-powerful, the mechanical world of physical forces led to the notion of God's attribute of being all-forceful. With this shift in meaning, the power of God in the medium of language was concealed, and this eclipse of divine power eventually extended into all areas of society where force became the only means of dealing with relationships, whether these relationships were to nature or to other human beings. So today, the hallmark of our relationship to nature is force. Likewise, the standard of our relationship to other persons has become force, spilling over quite often into raw violence.

In this context, power has totally lost its meaning. Power has much more in common with love and respect than it does with force and violence. Power draws people into agreement; force coerces them into obedience. We are not thereby maintaining that force is never necessary in an imperfect world, but it should only be used when power has clearly failed. That is to say, in human relationships, whether on an individual, a national or an international level, the use of force is always a tacit admission of failure. Had we been powerful enough, the force would not have been necessary. As an American citizen, I am not ready to admit failure. I am not ready to concede that we are a powerless nation, that we have nothing left in reserve except raw violence. I am still convinced that we can discover the true power of words, that we can regain the power of dialogue and diplomacy, and that we can recover a moral authority, which flows out of authentic power. Since moral authority is an authentic expression of power, the following chapters will undertake to analyze our current situation and to search for moral guideposts that could point us onto the right path.

At the outset of our discussion, we must distinguish between the *legal*, the *moral* and the *religious*. The "legal" in the context of our investigation refers to the federal and state laws and regulations that are necessary in order to ensure a stable and safe society. Criminal law, for instance, deals with acts of intentional harm to individuals of the society; some protection must be provided against harmful acts that can range from vandalism to murder. On the other hand, civil law deals with disputes between private parties such as divorces, child support, breach of contract and so forth. Thanks to the legal structure of a country, its citizens are protected from harm and afforded an environment in which they can pursue their professional and personal interests.

The "moral" in a society concerns certain standards of behavior that are considered right or just. In everyday conversation, morality and ethics are often used synonymously, but technically speaking, ethics is a more systematized approach to right and wrong conduct. The code of conduct governing the medical profession, for instance, is termed "medical ethics", and in a similar vein, there is usually a prescribed set of values for the behavior of individuals within a particular religious group. There is, for example, the discipline of Christian ethics that investigates systematically the implications of Christian faith for individual conduct and for social engagement. In contrast to ethics, the "moral" in society is more diffused and more closely related to the mores of the culture. The accepted customs, the behavioral values, the perception of right and wrong in given situations—all of this makes up the morality of the society. From this, it should be apparent that the "moral" and the "ethical" are not always identical. What is considered to be acceptable behavior in society as a whole may not accord with the ethical values of a particular religion, and this will be especially true in a pluralistic society, characterized by diverse religious views which may range from an unbending fundamentalism to a staunch atheism. That particular religious groups may not be satisfied with the basic moral attitudes of the society is, therefore, to be expected, but in a pluralistic society, it is imperative that we agree on certain moral values so that we can engage in productive dialogue. If our differences are greater than our agreements, we cannot survive. If the divisiveness of a nation is deeper than the common convictions of its citizens, it will eventually implode.

Just as the morality of a modern, pluralistic society will never be identical with the ethical views of a particular religion, so also federal and state laws will never reflect totally the morality of society. Nor would such an identity between the legal and the moral even be desirable. It is not the purpose of the law to make saints out of ordinary citizens, but rather to prevent them from becoming demons. Particularly in times of moral uncertainty in a society, legislators should be very cautious about incorporating moral values into law. Where there is no general consensus about moral conduct in a specific area, considerable restraint should be exercised by lawmakers. On the other hand, there is no doubt that an absolute separation of the legal and the moral is not only impossible, but also equally as undesirable as the identity of the two. Consider murder, for instance. It is not only immoral, but also illegal. It not only offends our moral sensitivities, it renders organized society impossible. Clearly, there is an overlapping of morality and legality, but this in no way justifies the attempt of some conservatives to force their moral views on the whole of society through legal means.

Since we are searching for moral guideposts for concerned citizens, we will focus in the following chapters on neither the legal nor the religious, but rather on the moral dimension in society. To this end, we pose the question: what guideposts for moral conduct can be discovered that might be acceptable to society as a whole regardless of religious persuasion? Although we will not proceed on the basis of particular religious beliefs, the experience of transcendence in the broadest sense must be assumed if we are to avoid a moral nihilism. If there is no difference between "is" and "ought", between "what-we-are" and "what-we-should-be", if there is absolutely nothing that transcends the present situation, then we are left with no basis whatsoever for moral judgment. Unfortunately, this is more or less the state of affairs today in American society. The eclipse of power in society is paralleled by the eclipse of the eternal in the individual's experience of time, leaving him with no foundation for moral judgment. The atheist may well object at this point that religion is being surreptitiously introduced in order to avoid the dilemma of moral nihilism, but in actual fact, the relationship between time and eternity is first and foremost a philosophical, not a religious matter. As I pointed out in *Citizens of the Broken Compass*, philosophers from Plato and Aristotle down to Martin Heidegger and Alfred North Whitehead have struggled to understand how time and eternity are related to each other. Even Friedrich Nietzsche who was professedly atheistic struggled with the problem of time and eternity and finally introduced the concept of the eternal into his philosophical reflection on morality. What is different about Western societies today is this: we don't struggle with the problem anymore!

The eternal has been eclipsed in our experience of time so that we perceive only the here and now, and this myopic view of reality does not allow tradition in any form to come into clear focus. Notice how easily we have abandoned 2500 years of tradition with regard to the institution of marriage or how numb we have become to the slaughter of human lives at home and abroad. Western culture has become one-dimensional, meaning that it lacks the element of transcendence necessary for a moral orientation in time. It is, as though we have been set adrift at sea on a stormy night without a compass, and lacking any point of orientation, we are incapable of making sound moral judgments. All possible modes of conduct appear equally valid or invalid, equally moral or immoral because we find no basis for making a decision one way or the other. The religious conservative may argue that he is not affected by the moral nihilism of our times and that he has a firm foundation, for instance, in the Christian Bible. But the fundamentalist's literal interpretation of the Bible, his rigid position on moral issues, and his utter inability to enter into constructive dialogue with those of opposing opinions reflect an existential insecurity that is caused by the eclipse of the eternal in time. The desperate clinging to fixed moral standards of times past has very little to do with an appreciation of tradition. As the Latin word "traditio" indicates, tradition is in essence a process. Far from being static, tradition is the "handing over" or the "delivery" of something, and when a society seriously lives out of its tradition, it is continually involved in the process of delivering something from the past into the present. Forcing fixed values of the past onto the present is more akin to acts of violence than to the creative process of tradition. The creative process of tradition is, however, not possible when time is severed from eternity. Only in the existential moment of the eternal in time is an Archimedes' point found that allows a creative transmission of the old into the new.

Having distinguished between the concepts of the legal, the moral and the religious, it remains to concede that these distinctions are necessarily only present in a modern or post-modern society and that other cultures, particularly more primitive ones, have functioned quite well without them. If we consider, for example, an ancient culture of the Middle East, we will soon discover that the legal, the moral and the religious build a unified whole. When the ancient Israelites were first confronted with the Ten Commandments, no one would have come upon the idea of asking whether these were communal laws, moral precepts or religious duties. Clearly, the Second Table of the Commandments comprises more or less the necessary and minimum requirements for living together in a society. No group can sustain itself for very long if murder, theft and so forth are not prohibited. Still, the ancient Israelites did not distinguish these legal requirements from their religious duties. Their experience was holistic, and their society was much more uniform than ours.

We might indeed wish that modern Western societies were as straightforward as the ones of the ancient world. Perhaps deep inside of every one of us, there is a nostalgic longing for a time past when the legal, the moral and the religious formed, if not a unified whole, at least a harmonious pattern. But the notion of turning back the clock to a former time when life seemed simpler and moral values were clearer is, to put it bluntly, an illusion. Some Americans may not like the pluralistic society in which they live, but it is for better or worse here to stay—at least for the foreseeable future—, and the attempts of many conservatives to return to the apparent simplicity of the 1950s will only create a further divide in their country. Between the 1950s and 2015 stands the cultural revolution of the 1960s with the Civil Rights Act, the founding of the National Organization of Women and the Stonewall Riots for gay/lesbian rights. Regardless of one's political, ethical or religious views, these historical events cannot be simply erased, and we ignore them at our own peril. If conservatives really want to be constructive, they need to accept this history as in some way *their* history, to engage the thoughts and aims of these movements and to search for a common ground that will allow them to move forward and to heal the divisiveness in their country. In my opinion, it is incumbent upon conservatives and liberals alike to recognize this undeniable fact: moral authority cannot be coerced, it must be cultivated.

Chapter 2

Divine Law, Natural Law
and the Laws of Nature

In our search for the moral dimension in modern and post-
modern Western societies, it behooves us to consider at the
outset several pre-modern societies in which the moral aspect
was more evident. Living as we do in a situation of moral disorientation, it should be very instructive to discover how societies
at other times and in other places have experienced the moral
dimension and to inquire about the possibility of "delivering"
some of their insights into our present situation. For this
purpose, we turn our attention to the concept of *law*.

If we look at the ancient Israelite society of the first
millennium BC or at the classical Greek and Roman societies of
roughly the same period, we notice at once that our distinctions
between the legal, the moral and the religious do not apply. In the
Hebrew language of the first millennium BC between the time of
the United Kingdom and the Exile, there were several words that
were used in referring to law; roughly transliterated, these were:
torah (meaning: "instruction", "guidance" or "direction"), *miswah*
("commandment"), *dabhar* ("word"), *hoq* ("decree", "precept")
and *mispat* ("judgment", "ordinance" or "custom"). Of these
words, it was *torah* that finally became primary as a designation
for law in the broadest sense. So when we read in the Book of
Deuteronomy chapter 1 verse 5: "Beyond the Jordan, in the land
of Moab, Moses undertook to explain this law...", the word for
"law" in the Hebrew text is *torah*, and it apparently referred to the
whole body of Israelite law including civil, criminal and ritual
ordinances. Nevertheless, it would be a mistake to limit our
understanding of law to the occurrences of *torah* in the Hebrew
text since this word only gained prominence over a period of

11

time. In the Book of Exodus chapter 18 verse 16, *torah* occurs in a parallel construction with *hoq*, and in this context, it is clear that only civil law is under consideration. We read:

> On the morrow Moses sat to judge the people, and the people stood about Moses from morning till evening. When Moses' father-in-law saw all that he was doing for the people, he said, "What is this that you are doing for the people? Why do you sit alone, and all the people stand about you from morning till evening?" And Moses said to his father-in-law, "Because the people come to me to inquire of God; when they have a dispute, they come to me and I decide between a man and his neighbor, and I make them know the precepts (*hoq*) of God and His laws (*torah*).

Particularly interesting in this passage is the idea that all of the laws and ordinances governing civil matters were given by God. That is, the idea of God and the concept of law were inseparable in the minds of the ancients; the modern concept of a secular law was at that time unknown.

If we consider the various sections in the Hebrew Bible where law is presented and discussed, we discover that the Israelites had basically two types of law: the categorical law as exemplified in the Ten Commandments (Exodus 20.2–17 and Deuteronomy 5.6–21) and the casuistic law as found in the so-called Covenant Code (Exodus 20.22–23.33). With the exception of the Sabbath command and the command to honor parents, the Ten Commandments are stated in negative form without mention of consequences for non-compliance. For instance, it is stated categorically: "You shall not kill", without specifying the punishment for manslaughter or murder. On the other hand, the casuistic laws typically take the logical form of "If...then" statements. For instance, we read in the Book of Exodus chapter 22 verse 5: "When a man causes a field or vineyard to be grazed over, or lets his beast loose and it feeds in another man's field, he shall make restitution from the best in his own field and in his own vineyard."

Defining features of the Israelite understanding of law include not only the fact that civil, criminal and ritual ordinances were considered to be of divine original, but also that the whole of the law was understood in the context of the *covenant* with God. As the biblical scholar Walter Harrelson once noted: "The covenant between God and Israel at the holy mountain (Exodus 19–24) provided the foundation for all Israelite law."[2(p80)] It was precisely in the context of this covenant relationship that the Israelites understood the categorical commandments. If there is a covenant between God and a group of people, then God is in a position to specify unqualifiedly the conditions of this covenant. It is God's to command and Israel's to obey. If we apply the unqualified aspect of categorical law and the "If...then" structure of casuistic law to natural phenomena, we begin to get a glimpse of the way in which the concept of the laws of nature developed. To be more explicit: there is little doubt that the modern concept of the laws of nature has its roots in the religious tradition, and it was not until the second half of the second millennium AD that the notion of law finally lost its religious connotations and emerged as a purely scientific concept.

Although the primary usage of the Hebrew terms for law focused on the civil, moral and ritual ordinances necessary for life in the community, there are scattered passages in the Hebrew Bible, particularly in the later books known as the Wisdom literature, in which the word *hoq* is used in reference to nature itself. In the Book of Proverbs, wisdom is personified as a prophetess who speaks these words:

When he (God) established the heavens, I was there, when he drew a circle on the face of the deep, when he made firm the skies above, when he established the fountains of the deep,

when he gave to the sea its decree (hoq), so that the waters might not transgress his command, when he marked out the foundations of the earth, then I was beside him, like a master workman... (Italics added)
Proverbs 8.27–29

A similar usage of the word *hoq* occurs in the Book of Job:

God understands the way to it (wisdom), and he knows its place. For he looks to the ends of the earth, and sees everything under the heavens. When he gave to the wind its weight, and meted out the waters by measure; when he made a decree *(hoq)* for the rain, and a way for the lightning of the thunder; then he saw it and declared it; he established it, and searched it out.
Job 28.23–27

In these passages, it is evident that God the Lawgiver, who has given the law and the ordinances to Israel for her communal life, has also given the physical world certain laws and decrees. In all likelihood, this idea could not have been developed until the Israelites came to think of their God as creator of the world, but as soon as God the Lawgiver was also understood to be God the Creator, the application of law to physical phenomena was a very natural transition in thought. In both of the aforementioned passages, the Hebrew word *hoq* is translated in the Latin Bible (Vulgate) as *lex*, i.e. as "law". According to the Austrian philosopher and sociologist Edgar Zilsel, we observe in these passages the oldest stage in the development of the modern concept of the laws of nature.[3(p69)]

To be sure, it was a long way from the primitive ideas of the Biblical writers to the modern concept of science, but nevertheless the similarities between the two are undeniable. The idea that the sea *obeys* the command of God must have been based on the empirical observation that the sea, although threatening and stormy at times, remains within it bounds. Furthermore, there was an element of *constraint* in the movement of the sea that paralleled the human experience of obedience, and finally, the *regularity* of the sea's movement found its counterpart in the constancy of the Torah. When we add to these observations the insight of depth psychology concerning the symbolic value of the sea, i.e. the insight that the sea is a symbol of the unconscious — one thinks here of C. G. Jung —, we can easily understand how the ancients made the transition from the laws of the community to the laws of nature. Just as disorder in society could destroy the life of the community, chaos in nature could plunge the creation into the abyss. In both realms, a law was necessary in order to ensure stability and safety, and in both realms, it was God who provided the law. Nowhere could it be more evident that the modern concept of the laws of nature has its roots in the religious, albeit mythological, thinking of primitive cultures.

If we turn our attention away from the ancient Hebrew culture to classical Greek society of the eighth century BC, we discover ideas similar to those in the Wisdom literature of the Israelites. The poems of Hesiod deal with the origin of the universe, with the relationship between humans and the gods, and with the social order of society. In his poem *Works and Days*, Hesiod writes:

Listen now to justice, and forget,
completely, violence.
For Cronus' son set up
this law for men.
Fish, flesh, and fowl
each other may devour,
for right is not in them.
But right he gave
to men, and this
is best by far.[4(p18)]

According to Greek mythology, Zeus, the son of Cronus, was the head of the Olympian gods and the supreme lawgiver. So Zeus determined that the law of devouring and being devoured would apply to nature, whereas the law of justice would be established among human beings.[5(p52)]

In the sixth century BC, a comprehensive conformity with natural law seems to be reflected in the well-known saying of Anaximander, which has come down to us through Simplicius: "Into those things from which existing things have their coming into being, their passing away, too, takes place, according to what must be; *for they make reparation to one another for their injustice according to the ordinance of time.*"[4(p34)] This entire passage is very obscure, but the italicized portion, which is the Anaximander fragment, has become famous because it is the only surviving sentence of his work on the nature of things. Anaximander, as well as many other early Greek philosophers, thought that the things of nature were composed of opposites: the hot and the cold, the dry and the moist and so forth. These opposites are "those things from which existing things have their coming into being", and when these opposites are disorderly, they must make reparation for their injustice. In his commentary on this passage, John Mansley Robinson denotes Anaximander's idea as the "law of compensation" and attempts to explain it by giving an everyday example. "But what is the necessity that compels the opposites to make reparation to one another for their injustice? One thing is certain: the roots of our confidence in the law of compensation lie deep in human nature. We feel 'instinctively' that an unusually mild autumn will have to be 'paid for' by an unusually severe winter."[4(p36)] In referring to the injustice of nature, Anaximander uses the same Greek word that is used in other contexts for moral injustice (*adikia*), thus giving expression to an overarching view of law and justice that embraces nature as well as human conduct and communal living. A similar thought is expressed by Heraclitus around 500 BC: "The sun will not overstep his measures; for if he does, the Furies, defenders of Justice, will find him out."[4](p92) In Greek mythology, the Furies were the female goddesses of vengeance, and in this passage, Heraclitus indicates that they would punish the sun if it were to transgress its bounds. In the classical philosophy that followed in the late fifth and fourth centuries BC, these ideas about law and nature were not further developed. In fact, in the philosophies of Plato and Aristotle, law and nature tended to be understood as contrasting ideas; according to them, laws were promulgated by human beings and were considered to be independent of nature.[5](p51–2)

Unlike Plato and Aristotle, however, the Stoic philosophers, beginning with Zeno around 300 BC, continued the tradition of the pre-Socratic philosophers and developed the idea of *natural law*, which later became a fundamental concept of medieval Europe. From Heraclitus, the Stoics took over the notion of the *logos* or "reason", which was thought to permeate the entire universe and to direct all events, natural and human. Cleanthes, the successor of Zeno in the Athenian school, wrote a *Hymn to Zeus* in which he expresses these views:

Most majestic of immortals, many-titled, ever omnipotent Zeus, prime mover of nature (*physis*), who with your law (*nomos*) steer all things, hail to you. For it is proper for any mortal to address you: we are your offspring, and alone of all mortal creatures which are alive and tread the earth we bear a likeness to god. Therefore I shall hymn you and sing for ever of your might. All this cosmos, as it spins around the earth, obeys you, whichever way you lead, and willingly submits to your sway. Such is the double-edged fiery ever-living thunderbolt which you hold at the ready in your unvanquished hands. For under its strokes all the works of nature (*physis*) are accomplished. With it you direct the universal reason (*logos*) which runs through all things and intermingles with the lights of heaven both great and small.[6](p326)

The occurrence of the Greek words *physis* ("nature"), *nomos* ("law") and *logos* ("reason") in this text is characteristic of Stoic thought. The law that permeates all nature *is* reason, and nature is required to function according to the dictates of reason. The fact that this law is also a *moral* law dictating what is right and wrong conduct among humans comes to expression in the following sentence of the hymn: "(Everlasting reason) is shunned and neglected by the bad among mortal men, the wretched, who ever yearn for the possession of goods yet neither see nor hear god's universal law (*nomos*), by obeying which they could lead a good life in partnership with intelligence."[6(p327)] So the universal law that permeates all things is both the law of natural occurrences and the moral law of human conduct. In contrast to Plato and Aristotle, the Stoics refused to draw a clear distinction between the legal/moral realm of human beings and the realm of nature. The Stoic natural law is comprehensive.

In describing the natural law of the cosmos, terminology of the Stoics reflects a certain ambiguity that is of primary importance for the history of the concept. In some passages, we read that the natural law *permeates* the universe like an extremely fine material substance, which is called the "ether". In other passages, however, the natural law is said to be *dictated* to nature in the same way that a god would impose his commands on human beings. This wavering between an understanding of natural law as *immanent* or as *imposed* was probably not recognized by the Stoics themselves. On the one hand, we have a law that is *in* nature itself and cannot be separated from nature. Nature without this law would no longer be nature. That is, the law is constitutive for nature. If we consider the relationships expressed in a particular law, then these relations would be internal to nature itself. On the other hand, natural law as imposed is external to nature, and all of the relationships expressed in the law are external to the natural occurrences themselves. Without the imposed natural law, nature would remain unchanged because the relationships under consideration are external to nature and thus in no way constitutive of it.

Let us consider an example out of the third century BC. Although the Greeks did not develop the concept of the laws of nature in the modern sense, they did discover three regularities in nature that we would term laws: the lever principle, the principle of buoyancy and the optical law of reflection. All three of these were known by Archimedes of Syracuse (287–212 BC), and in his writings, he developed them mathematically in the form of theorems. If we consider the principle of buoyancy—the principle actually discovered by Archimedes himself—, the distinction between *imposed law* and *immanent law* can be explained in this way. According to the principle of buoyancy, there is a relationship between the density of an object and the amount of water that it displaces when submerged so that objects of greater density sink and ones of lesser density float. Assuming that this is an imposed law, neither the water nor the object would change if the law were somehow eliminated. But if the law is immanent, the nature of both the water and the object depend on the relationship of buoyancy. In this simple case, most people will agree that the law is imposed, whether by God or by human intelligence. However, if we ask the same question about the immanence or imposition of law in the case of the Higgs particle (which is the subject of scientific investigation in the "European Council for Nuclear Research" in Geneva, Switzerland), the particle physicist will probably explain to us that the mass of other elementary particles and therefore the entire structure of nature depend on their relationship to the Higgs particle. As we shall see later, the ambiguity between immanence and imposition of natural law prevailed until the advent of modern science in the seventeenth century when the notion of imposed law on nature became dominant. According to Sir Isaac Newton, for instance, the laws of nature are imposed by God, and therefore any irregularities in the movement of the heavenly bodies must be corrected by the action of God.

The difference between imposed and immanent natural law is also significant in the moral realm. Consider the prohibition against murder. Is this prohibition an imposed law that could be changed without any fundamental change to society? Or is it immanent in the notion of society itself so that society cannot be *society* without it? One can raise the same question about the prohibition against incest or about the rules of marriage. If all such moral laws are thought to have been imposed in former times by the human intellect, then they might well seem to be arbitrary and unnecessary in a modern society. Perhaps our ancestors believed that these moral laws were imposed by God. If so, there would be no convincing reason for retaining them in an atheistic society. As Nietzsche once noted, if you eliminate the Lawgiver, you eliminate the Law. In short, if moral laws are imposed by humans, then humans should be able to change them as they please. On the other hand, the immanence of such laws in society would mean that society itself would dissolve if these laws were removed. This is indeed a disconcerting thought, but one that we should take very seriously. In Western societies today, there is almost universal agreement that all moral laws are imposed, but there is no way to establish the validity of this assumption without removing the laws and observing the consequences. In the physical realm, no physicist would want to remove the Higgs field from the universe in order to observe the consequences, but in the moral realm, we have glibly removed moral restraints decade after decade as though no consequences would follow.

The Stoic idea of natural law was taken over by Cicero in the first century BC and presented in a form that could be easily transmitted into Christian thought of the Middle Ages. Written around 51 BC, Cicero's *On the Laws* (*De Legibus*) offers in Book I the fullest exposition of the Stoic idea of natural law that we possess today. When we use the word "law", we usually mean the laws of the state, i.e. written laws that are formulated and promulgated by legislators and that are enforced by the judiciary, but before any state was constituted or any law was written, there was, according to Cicero, the highest law in nature. He writes:

Philosophers have taken their starting point from law; and they are probably right to do so if, as these same people define it, *law is the highest reason, rooted in nature*, which commands things that must be done and prohibits the opposite. When this same reason is secured and established in the human mind, it is law.[7](1.18) (Italics added)

In this passage, Cicero identifies law with reason and explains that reason is "rooted in nature" and "established in the human mind"; the reason in nature and the reason in the human mind are the same, and Cicero refers to both as the highest law. Since this law permeates all things, it binds all people together into a common world city:

What is there, not just in humans, but in all heaven and earth, more divine than reason? When it has matured and come to perfection, it is properly named wisdom. And therefore, since there is nothing better than reason, reason forms the first bond between human and god. And those who share reason also share right reason; and since that is law, we humans must be considered to be closely allied to gods by law. Furthermore, those who share law also share the procedures of justice; and those who have these things in common must be considered members of the same state, all the more so if they obey the same commands and authorities. Moreover, they do obey this celestial order, the divine mind and the all-powerful god, so that this whole cosmos must be considered to be the common state of gods and humans.[7](1.22f)

Although the entire universe shares in the law of nature, human beings have a privileged position because in them reason has become *right* reason, which allows them to distinguish between right and wrong, just and unjust and thus to make morally correct decisions. Cicero's comments about the bond of reason between human beings and the gods may seem strange to modern ears, but one should note that he is arguing in line with the Stoics about the character of the universe, not about the necessity or desirability of religious faith. The point is purely philosophical: all things in the universe are connected through reason, i.e. through natural law (*lex naturalis*). According to Cicero, this natural law is implanted in the soul of the individual, and anyone who acts against the dictates of right reason "will be in exile from himself".[8(3.33)] Expressed in modern terms: *acting immorally results in self-estrangement*. Through immoral conduct, we deny something within ourselves.

Finally, the presence of natural law in the minds of all human beings is the basis of their common nature, and because of this common nature all men and women are equally capable of living a virtuous life, i.e. living in accordance with the law of nature. Unfortunately, the word "virtue" has almost lost any real meaning in the English language, and it is difficult today for us to understand what Cicero and others meant when they employed the term. In the translation of classical texts into English, there has been a tendency to replace the word "virtue" with "excellence" in order to capture the meaning of the Greek *arete*, which corresponds to the Latin *virtus*. The virtuous life is the excellent life — the life in which individuals develop their best natural talents and abilities. It would be a mistake, however, to think that attaining the excellent life is a purely individual matter. If all human beings share a common nature and if they are all bound together into one common world city, then acting morally in accordance with natural law will be synonymous with acting in the interest of the common good. The enlightened citizen will realize that the individual cannot attain the life of excellence unless he strives for the common good of the world city. The connectivity of all things means that we do not live just for ourselves as the libertarians insist. Cicero agrees with Plato that we live to a great extent for those around us, for family and friends, and for the society in which we find ourselves. The words of Cicero on this matter are impressive:

> We are not born for ourselves alone, to use Plato's splendid words, but our country claims for itself one part of our birth, and our friends another. Moreover, as the Stoics believe, everything produced on the earth is created for the use of humankind, and *human beings are born for the sake of human beings, so that they may be able to assist one another.* Consequently, we ought in this to follow nature as our leader, to contribute to the community "common benefits" (*communes utilitates*), and, by the exchange of dutiful services, by giving and receiving expertise and effort and means, to bind fast the fellowship of all human beings with each other.[9](1.22) (Italics added)

By contributing to the common good of society, we conform to the natural law, and as a result, we are able to attain the life of excellence.

The Stoic understanding of nature in general and of human nature in particular was—to use the technical term—*teleological*. This means that human nature is directed toward some goal and is shaped by some purpose. Unlike the views of many modern (Jean Paul Sartre) and post-modern (Michel Foucault) philosophers who maintain that human existence has no inherent direction or goal, the Stoics claimed that humans are by nature directed toward a specific end or goal. Around the middle of the third century AD, Diogenes Laertius reports the classical views of the Stoics in this way:

Therefore Zeno in his book *On the nature of man* was the first to say that living in agreement with nature is the end, which is living in accordance with virtue. For nature leads us towards virtue... Further, living in accordance with virtue is equivalent to living in accordance with experience of what happens by nature, as Chrysippus says in *On ends* book I: for our own natures are parts of the nature of the whole. Therefore, living in agreement with nature comes to be the end, which is in accordance with the nature of oneself and that of the whole, engaging in no activity wont to be forbidden by the universal law, which is the right reason pervading everything and identical to Zeus, who is this director of the administration of existing things.[6(p395)]

Once again, we see the ambiguity between Zeus as director of all existing things and the universal law that permeates all things. But more importantly, we see in this passage that the goal or end of human existence is to live in accordance with one's own nature and the nature of the universe. On first reading, one might interpret this passage in a purely libertarian or hedonistic fashion; living in accordance with one's own nature would mean, in this case, to set self-preservation and the maximization of individual pleasure as the highest goal of human existence. What the Stoics understood by the phrase "in accordance with nature" was, however, something quite different. By gaining insight into the natural law of the cosmos, the individual comes to the realization that true happiness is only possible when he focuses on the common good. Individual happiness apart from the welfare of society as a whole is for the Stoics an illusion. Thus, living according to one's nature does not mean indulging the most primitive impulses of self-preservation and sensual pleasure, but rather finding one's place within the all-embracing rational, harmonious structure of nature.[10(3.16–26)] If one indeed succeeds in attaining this goal, one has attained true virtue, the life of excellence, a fulfilled life of harmony, the highest goal of human existence.

In the early decades of the first century AD, the Stoic idea of natural law was adopted by Christian thinkers who were addressing a non-Jewish audience. It is well known that Jesus himself never extended his ministry beyond the boundaries of his Jewish homeland and that the first "Christian" church in Jerusalem was considered to be one of the Jewish sects in the region. Furthermore, the message that Jesus left behind after his death was inseparably connected with the concept of Jewish law, as is evidenced, for instance, in the Sermon on the Mount. Here we read:

Think not that I (Jesus) have come to abolish the law and the prophets; I have come not to abolish them but to fulfil them. For truly, I say to you, till heaven and earth pass away, not an iota, not a dot, will pass from the law until all is accomplished. Whoever then relaxes one of the least of these commandments and teaches men so, shall be called least in the kingdom of heaven; but he who does them and teaches them shall be called great in the kingdom of heaven.
Matthew 5.17–19

"The law and the prophets" in this passage refers to the first two sections of the Hebrew Bible, the third section being "the writings". As long as the early Christian church remained a Jewish sect, the orientation of its message to the Torah was not only unproblematic, but totally in line with the tradition. However, the spread of the Christian message to non-Jewish regions extending West as far as Rome presented the leaders of the new religion with the following problem: since the message of Jesus was bound up with Jewish law, it was unclear whether this message had any significance for men and women who understood very little about Jewish law and who felt in any case no obligation to obey it. As we know from the writings of the Apostle Paul, the Stoic idea of natural law provided the key to making this transition. In writing to the Christians in Rome, Paul combines "law" with "nature" and refers to the "conscience", which was also a typically Stoic idea. In Romans chapter 2 verses 14–15, he writes:

> When the Gentiles who have not the law (Torah) do by *nature* what the law (Torah) requires, they are a law (natural law) to themselves, even though they do not have the law (Torah). They show that what the law requires is written on their hearts, while their conscience also bears witness...

The idea of an unwritten natural law, which dictates to the conscience what is right and wrong, became a cornerstone in Christian theology and found its classical formulation in the writings of Thomas Aquinas in the thirteenth century.

With the integration of the old Stoic notion of natural law into the Christian tradition, there was, however, a noticeable shift in emphasis that had a later impact on the science of the seventeenth century. Although the Stoics seemed to waver between an understanding of natural law as immanent and as imposed, their materialistic view of law as a quasi-substance permeating nature definitely favored the immanent side of the ambiguity. In contrast, the concept of God's law in the Judeo-Christian tradition was clearly based on the notion of imposition so that this side of the Stoic ambiguity became prominent in Christian theology and remained more or less the standard understanding of nature down to the seventeenth century. So when Sir Isaac Newton developed his classical concepts of physics in the seventeenth century, he could hold firmly to the conviction that God imposed laws on nature just as He imposed laws on human beings and human society.

Still, the continuity of thought between the Middle Ages and dawn of modern science was not as clear as our description might suggest. It is true that Newton and other scientists of the period embraced from the Middle Ages the concept of imposed law in the human and the physical realm, but in both realms, they understood the imposed law differently than their medieval predecessors had. For the scientists, the imposed law in the human realm became identified with written documents such as the Torah, and the imposed law in the realm of nature was thought to be empirically discoverable and mathematically expressible. In both cases, we observe a reductionistic tendency that has had important consequences for our understanding of law. As soon as the imposed law in the human realm lost its cosmic dimension and became identified with particular writings, a literalistic interpretation of these writings developed that was quite unknown in previous ages. At this point, we see the beginnings of the fundamentalist notion of verbal inspiration of the Bible; God's law is now thought to be fixed permanently in a particular document. Similarly, the imposed law in the realm of nature lost its universal character and became identified with particular mathematical formulations, i.e. with specific laws; the *law* of nature became the *laws* of nature.

If any remnant of the immanent idea of law in nature had remained in the pre-scientific theological tradition, it was certainly discarded when scientists like Galileo and Newton adopted the atomism of the Epicureans as the foundation of their investigation. The Epicurean atoms were self-contained, indestructible entities that could only enter into external relations. If we look for an analogy to the Stoic and the Epicurean concepts of nature, we can say that the Stoics thought of nature as a membrane, whereas the Epicureans conceived of nature as a huge collection of marbles. The Stoic "membrane" was permeated by *natural law*, whereas the Epicurean "marbles" were independent entities whose external relationships would henceforth be termed the *laws of nature*. So the original unity of the

Stoic natural law was disrupted, and the way was open for a *literalist* interpretation of law in the human realm as well as an *empiricist* understanding of law in nature. These two interpretations of law eventually gave rise to the present-day religious fundamentalist and the atheistic scientist.

The process that we have just described, whereby the *law* of nature became the *laws* of nature, began in the seventeenth century and was completed sometime during the eighteenth century, although historians of science disagree about the exact dates. There is an isolated reference to the "laws of nature" in the works of Johannes Kepler, but it was in the writings of Kepler's British contemporary Sir Francis Bacon that we observe the new concept of the laws of nature emerging with real clarity.[5(p68)] Francis Bacon was born in 1561 in England, and according to his biographers, he was a very gifted child, being admitted at the early age of twelve into Trinity College in Cambridge. Strictly speaking, Bacon did not become a scientist in the usual sense; he had no laboratory and made no discoveries as Kepler and Galileo conversely had. Nevertheless, he is considered one of the founders of modern science because he was the first to recognize the importance of method for scientific inquiry. In his work entitled *The New Organon or True Directions Concerning the Interpretation of Nature* (1620), Bacon laid out an alternative to the traditional method of logic as handed down in Aristotle's *Organon*. Whereas Aristotle's methods of logic were deductive, Bacon's new method of scientific inquiry was inductive. Bacon's method was designed to discover new truths about nature; Aristotle's was only useful as a tool to draw new conclusions from old truths. The key to Bacon's new method was the interplay of rational thought and experimentation. In Aphorism 95 of Book I, he writes:

Those who have handled sciences have been either men of experiment or men of dogmas. The men of experiment are like the ant, they only collect and use; the reasoners resemble spiders, who make cobwebs out of their own substance. But the bee takes a middle course: it gathers its material from the flowers of the garden and of the field, but transforms and digests it by a power of its own. Not unlike this is the true business of philosophy; for it neither relies solely or chiefly on the powers of the mind, nor does it take the matter which it gathers from natural history and mechanical experiments and lay it up in the memory whole, as it finds it, but lays it up in the understanding altered and digested. Therefore from a closer and purer league between these two faculties, the experimental and the rational (such as has never yet been made), much may be hoped.[11(1.95)]

For readers unfamiliar with seventeenth-century scientific writings, it may seem odd that Bacon refers to "philosophy" instead of "science", but this usage was very common at the time. At the close of the century, Robert Boyle was still designating his work as "experimental philosophy". In any case, Bacon hoped that scientists would be able to discover the true laws of nature through the use of his new method, and in Aphorism 17 of Book II, he himself speaks of "the law of heat" (*lex calidi*) and "the law of light" (*lex luminis*). These laws are derived from empirical observation and rational thought, but they are limited in scope to particular aspects of the physical world and have, therefore, very little in common with the Stoic notion of natural law.

Unlike many scientists of the seventeenth century who were devout Puritans, Francis Bacon seems to have had an ambivalent relationship to Christianity. He was reared by his mother who was a strict Puritan, but he himself never demonstrated much interest in religion as an adult. Nevertheless, certain basic Puritan ideas are unmistakable in his *New Organon*. As we read in Aphorism 93 of Book I, his hope for the future of modern science is based on his belief in divine providence:

The beginning is from God: for the business which is in hand, having the character of good so strongly impressed upon it, appears manifestly to proceed from God, who is the author of good, and the Father of Lights. Now in divine operations even the smallest beginnings lead of a certainty to their end. And as it was said of spiritual things, "The kingdom of God cometh not with observation," so is it in all the greater works of Divine Providence; everything glides on smoothly and noise-lessly, and the work is fairly going on before men are aware that it has begun. Nor should the prophecy of Daniel be forgotten touching the last ages of the world: "Many shall go to and fro, and knowledge shall be increased"; clearly intimating that the thorough passage of the world (which now by so many distant voyages seems to be accomplished, or in course of accomplishment), and the advancement of the sciences, are destined by fate, that is, by Divine Providence, to meet in the same age.[11(1.93)]

And in Aphorism 70 of Book I, he proposes that the creation of the world by God provides a pattern for proceeding with scientific experimentation:

Now God on the first day of creation created light only, giving to that work an entire day, in which no material substance was created. So must we likewise from experience of every kind first endeavor to discover true causes and axioms; and seek for experiments of Light, not for experiments of Fruit.[11(1.70)]

In these passages in which Bacon connects the laws of nature with the creation of the world by God, we can see that the Stoic idea of immanent law has been abandoned altogether. The laws of nature that are to be discovered through the new method of science are laws imposed by God at creation, and they involve only the external relations of individual entities.

Following the work of Francis Bacon, the French philosopher René Descartes published in 1644 his *Principles of Philosophy* (*Principia Philosophiae*) in which he set down among other things certain laws governing the motion of physical bodies. Descartes' First Law (*Prima lex naturae*) concerns the inertia of physical bodies, i.e. their property of remaining in their state of rest unless some external cause moves them. He writes:

> *The first law of nature: Each thing when left to itself continues in the same state; so once something is set in motion, it continues to move.* From God's immutability we can also know certain rules or laws of nature, which are the secondary and particular causes of the various motions we see in particular bodies.[12(2.37)]

Of particular interest for our discussion is the way in which Descartes arrives at his conclusion: it is the immutability of God that enables us to discover certain laws of nature. If, however, the laws of nature depend on the immutability of God, these laws cannot be immanent in nature itself. Furthermore, the laws of nature that can be known by human beings are only the secondary causes of motion. The primary cause of all motion is God himself. Finally, Descartes was convinced that God had created the universe with a certain quantity of motion and that He conserved this quantity throughout time. Descartes writes:

> It seems clear to me that the general cause (of motion) is no other than God himself. In the beginning he created matter, along with its motion and rest; and now, merely by regularly letting things run their course, he preserves the same amount of motion and rest in the material universe as he put there in the beginning.[12(2.36)]

As we can see, Descartes' version of the law of conservation is based on the notion that God imposed certain laws on nature and that these laws involve external relationships among bodies in motion.

Still, the undisputed scientific genius of the seventeenth century was neither Sir Francis Bacon nor René Descartes, but rather Sir Isaac Newton. The two major works of Newton that concern us are the *Principles of Mathematics* (*Principia Mathematica*, 1687) and the *Opticks* (1704). In his *Principles of Mathematics*, which he composed in Latin, Newton lays down his famous three laws of motion and designates them as *Lex I*, *Lex II* and *Lex III*; they are respectively the law of inertia, the law of force and the law of action/reaction.[13(2p13–14)] The laws of motion as formulated by Newton not only apply to the regularities of moving bodies on earth, but also to the movement of the heavenly bodies. It was the great achievement of Newton to provide a unified theory that could account for motion anywhere in the universe, and in this regard, he went far beyond the work of either Galileo or Kepler. In addition, the work of Newton concluded the process of transition from an Aristotelian understanding of matter to the Epicurean idea that all things are composed of tiny atoms. In his *Opticks*, he writes:

> All these things being considered, it seems probable to me, that God in the beginning formed matter in solid, massy, hard, impenetrable, moveable particles; of such sizes and figures, and with such other properties, and in such proportion to space, as most conduced to the end for which he formed them; and that these primitive particles being solids, are incomparably harder than any Porous bodies compounded of them; even so very hard, as never to wear or break in pieces: no ordinary power being able to divide what God himself made One, in the first creation.[14(p401)]

The solid, impenetrable atoms (Greek: *atomon*) were not only created by God; the Creator also imposed on them the laws of motion:

Now by the help of these Principles, all material Things seem to have been composed of the hard and solid Particles above-mention'd, variously associated in the first Creation by the Counsel of an intelligent Agent. For it became him who created them to set them in order. And if he did so, it's unphilosophical to seek for any other Origin of the World, or to pretend that it might arise out of a Chaos by the mere Laws of Nature; though being once form'd, it may continue by those Laws for many Ages.[14(p402)]

Finally, Newton reflects further on the fact that God imposed laws on nature and concludes that He could also alter these laws, if He wished:

And since Space is divisible in infinitum, and Matter is not necessarily in all places, it may be also allow'd that God is able to create Particles of Matter of several Sizes and Figures, and in several Proportions to Space, and perhaps of different Densities and Forces, and thereby to vary the Laws of Nature, and make Worlds of several sorts in several Parts of the Universe. At least, I see nothing of Contradiction in all this.[14(p403f)]

The new physics of Sir Isaac Newton presents us with a totally different picture of the world than that of the ancient Stoics. For the Stoics, natural law was most often understood as a principle of reason that permeated the universe; it was at once both a cosmic and a moral principle. If we look for a metaphor to describe the Stoic universe, we might well call it—as I have already suggested—an immense membrane in which everything is connected. In contrast, the universe of Newton was an assemblage of particles that are only related by the laws imposed on them by God. Metaphorically, we could say the Newtonian universe is a huge collection of billiard balls bouncing off of each other according to the imposed laws, but these balls are not really connected internally in any essential way. These billiard balls, i.e. atoms, have no properties beyond their mass, force and position, all of which can be quantified. Furthermore, the regularities of nature can be expressed by combining these properties into the proper mathematical formulae. From this, we can see that the universe has ceased to have any moral or ethical significance.

In the following century, one came to speak of the universe as the "Newtonian World Machine" — a huge mechanical universe, where every interaction was reduced to simple efficient cause and effect and where there was, therefore, no room for purposeful action. Since not even God could interrupt the chain of cause and effect, it was only logical that the whole idea of God would eventually be eliminated from this universe. In the eighteenth century, the German philosopher Immanuel Kant (1724–1804) accomplished this by substituting the concept of "pure reason" for Newton's idea of God. Significantly, Kant did not think of reason in the Stoic sense as the natural law permeating the universe, but rather in the modern sense as the rational, logical character of the human mind. Whereas Newton had maintained that *God* had imposed laws on nature, Kant insisted that it is the pure reason of the *human mind* that imposes laws on the manifold of human experience. According to Kant, there are no internal relations of regularity in nature itself that could be formulated into laws; the laws of nature are imposed on it by human beings.

Chapter 3

Overcoming Relativism

The transition from natural law to the laws of nature, as we have described in Chapter 2, has contributed significantly to the situation in which we find ourselves today—a situation that we can appropriately term "moral nihilism". The word "nihilism" can be used in various contexts with varying connotations, but by *moral* nihilism, we mean the situation in which a society can no longer find a reliable basis for establishing moral values and making moral decisions. After natural law had been transformed into the scientific laws of nature, nature itself was banned from moral discussion. When Immanuel Kant substituted the human mind for God as the necessary condition for imposing laws on nature, he did not intend to destroy the moral dimension, but rather to separate it from nature. His famous dictum about "the starry sky above us" and "the moral law within us" was aimed at preserving both a purely scientific understanding of nature and the moral dimension necessary for organized human societies. The first of these, i.e. the understanding of nature, he presented in his classic work *Critique of Pure Reason* (1781); the second, namely the moral dimension, found expression in his *Critique of Practical Reason* (1788). But there were multiple problems with Kant's approach.

Although he seems at first glance to place the physical and the moral perspectives next to each other in some harmonious fashion, they are, in fact, quite distinct from each other in his philosophy. On the one hand, we have the sphere of physics and the laws of nature; on the other hand, we have the sphere of ethics and human freedom. The laws of nature express the deterministic character of the world and have absolutely no bearing on the sphere of freedom in which human beings make ethical and moral decisions. Conversely, the ethical and moral decisions made in the sphere of freedom could not interrupt the causal nexus in the deterministic sphere of nature. In short, Kant's solution seemed to lack coherence. Nevertheless, the separation of human freedom from deterministic nature appeared to be the only way to preserve any discussion of morality in the face of modern science, as the closed causal nexus of the "Newtonian World Machine" not only excluded the intervention of God, but it also rendered human freedom impossible.

There was, however, a second development that we must consider in order to fully grasp the dilemma of moral nihilism. In the nineteenth century, the sphere of human freedom came to be identified more and more with the flow of history as distinct from the stream of natural occurrences in the physical world. Precisely because of their freedom to make decisions, human beings—in contrast to other animals—have a history. For human history is not simply a chronicle of events, that is, a list of dates and corresponding occurrences; essential to history are the intentions, motivations, values and decisions of human beings who are free agents. In religious traditions such as Judaism and Christianity, history was also thought to be directed toward some goal and therefore to have some purpose. Furthermore, certain ethical values were presented in these traditions as absolutely valid and unchanging, and the adherence to these values was thought to lead toward the desired goal of history. During the early decades of the nineteenth century, this teleological understanding of history continued to flourish parallel to the newer scientific understanding of the inorganic realm of nature. But it was inevitable that the scientific methods developed in the seventeenth century by Bacon, Galileo, Newton and others would eventually be applied to disciplines outside of pure physics and astronomy, and as soon as this took place, the traditional view of history was altered dramatically. An intermediate step in this process was the work of Charles Darwin and his new understanding of human beings.

Around the middle of the nineteenth century, Darwin applied scientific methods of inquiry to the realm of biology and developed the theory of the evolution of the species, published in *On the Origin of Species* (1859). The work of Darwin was revolutionary in many respects. Most importantly, Charles Darwin was the first scientist to extend systematically the methods of science into the organic realm of nature. The astronomy of Johannes Kepler and the physics of Sir Isaac Newton made little or no attempt to understand living organisms; these scientists were concerned with the movement and interaction of physical objects. Take the well-known anecdote about Newton and the falling apple. He may have been concerned about the cause of the apple's falling from the tree to the ground, but he was not particularly interested in the organic structure of the apple itself. When Darwin applied scientific thinking to living organisms, he was moving in a new direction, and he himself was well aware of the impact that this could have on Western societies. So in the beginning he proceeded very cautiously. On reading *On the Origin of Species*, one is struck by the fact that Darwin does not discuss the descent of humans at all. To be sure, there are plenty of conclusions that one can draw about the evolution of human beings, but his explicit treatment of the matter came later in the publication of *The Descent of Man* in 1871. Contrary to popular belief, Darwin did not suggest that human beings descended from apes, but rather that humans and apes have a common ancestor in the tree of evolution. What was damaging to the dignity of humankind was Darwin's assertion that there is no essential difference between human beings and animals—a point that he makes quite clear in his discussion of conscience. In Chapter 3, he writes:

I fully subscribe to the judgment of those writers who maintain that of all the differences between man and the lower animals, the moral sense or conscience is by far the most important....The following proposition seems to me in a high degree probable—namely, that any animal whatever, endowed with well-marked social instincts, would inevitably acquire a moral sense or conscience, as soon as its intellectual powers had become as well developed, or nearly as well developed, as in man.[15(p70-72)]

If there is no qualitative difference between human beings and animals, then the traditional understanding of the dignity of humankind and the special position of human beings in the order of nature and history becomes totally indefensible.

Once human beings had been subjected to scientific investigation, it was only a matter of time until history itself would be viewed as a subject of science. This occurred in the latter decades of the nineteenth century in a philosophical movement known as "historicism"—a movement that is associated primarily with the name of the German philosopher Wilhelm Dilthey. The so-called historicists applied the methods of scientific inquiry to the realm of history and discovered thereby that all moral and ethical values are relative to the period in which they were conceived. These new historians were convinced that history, like the physical sciences, is an empirical discipline and that it shares with the physical sciences the methods of observation and classification as well as the framing and testing of hypotheses.[16(p33f)] So they analyzed and dated ancient documents of historical interest and then classified them as business transactions, political documents, religious texts and so forth. Archeological discoveries were brought to bear in order to understand the documents in their proper contexts, and statistical methods along with comparative analysis were employed in order to shed new light on old documents.

In the area of biblical studies, Julius Wellhausen became well known after the publication of his *Israelite and Jewish History*

(1894) in which he developed a new critical theory of the origin and composition of the Pentateuch. According to the Graf-Wellhausen hypothesis, the five books of Moses were compiled from four different sources, written at different periods. In the mid-1960s, Herbert Hahn published a primer on Old Testament research in which he compared Wellhausen to Darwin:

His [Wellhausen's] position in Old Testament criticism is somewhat analogous to that of Darwin in the intellectual history of modern times... His [Wellhausen's] exposition was a prime example of the liberal approach to the exegesis of the Old Testament. Wellhausen omitted the theological interpretation entirely and emphasized the factor of *historical causation* instead. He consciously based his exposition on the *evolutionary view of history*.[17(p11–13)] (Italics added)

Just as Charles Darwin had developed an evolutionary view of the organic world, Julius Wellhausen presented an evolutionary view of history, applying the familiar methods of scientific inquiry and relying on the notion of historical causation. The results of this new approach to the study of history were groundbreaking.

Let us consider, for example, the first three chapters of the first Book of Moses (Genesis) in the Hebrew Bible. The methods of Wellhausen, which were based on a linguistic and statistical analysis of the text, indicated that these chapters contain two independent accounts of the creation of the world and that there is a break in the narrative at chapter 2, verse 4a. That is, the first creation account starts in chapter 1, verse 1 with the words: "In the beginning God created the heavens and the earth", and the second creation narrative begins in chapter 2, verse 4b, where we read: "In the day that the Lord God made the earth and the heavens..." Before the rise of modern historical methods, religious leaders had typically attempted to reconcile these two accounts, basing their approach on the belief that these three chapters must form a coherent whole if they are to lay any claim to truth. However, it is precisely the matter of *belief* that is excluded in any scientific inquiry into ancient documents. The scientific approach to history requires an objective stance analogous to the attitude of the chemist working in his laboratory.

Furthermore, the comparative methods of historicism require that these biblical accounts of creation be compared with other accounts stemming from the same region and approximately from the same period. One of our primary sources in this regard is the Babylonian creation epic, the so-called "Enuma Elish", named after the opening words of the text: "When on high (the heaven had not been named)".[18(p60)] This text was written in Old Babylonian on clay tablets sometime between 1800 and 1600 BC and has become known as the "Babylonian Genesis", since it presents an alternate account of creation. Comparing the content of the Babylonian creation account with the account in the Hebrew Bible, we are able to determine the characteristic beliefs of both the Babylonians and the Israelites. Although such comparisons can be extremely interesting, they have had an additional affect; they have led to a categorization of the first three chapters of Genesis as one of the creation myths of the Ancient Near East.

Our selection of a religious text out of the Hebrew Bible has highlighted another feature of historicism. Just as the laws of Newton were valid for interactions between bodies on earth as well as for the movement of the heavenly bodies, the methods of historicism were considered to be valid for the study of *all* historical documents, whether religious or secular. So both religious texts and political texts were subjected to the same critical analysis. If no text is considered to be sacrosanct, then the conclusions of the secular historian must be accepted in all cases. If the secular historian judges that the biblical account of the virgin birth of Jesus is a myth and that his walking on water is a legend, then these conclusions must be accepted by Christians as well as by non-Christians. Obviously, the development of historicism had a dramatic impact on religious communities such as the Christian Church and the Jewish Synagogue. Christian theology of the twentieth century was occupied to a great extent with the problem of understanding how a *religious* faith could be based on *secular* results. Stated succinctly, Christian faith demands an absolute commitment, but the historical understanding of the primary texts of Christianity is always relative. Nothing historical is ever absolute.

We have digressed somewhat into the area of religious texts in order to illustrate the problem of historicism, but for the purposes of the present investigation, the primary importance of historicism lies in the fact that it uncovered the *relativity of all moral values*. Not only are all religious ideas relative, but also all moral and ethical standards are relative. Since they are imbedded in a particular culture at a particular time, they may or may not have any validity in some other culture at some other time. In his discussion of historicism, H. P. Rickman summarized the situation well:

Historicism as a Weltanschauung does, indeed, carry alarming implications, for it raises the spectre of relativism which leads to nihilism. Our lives, in the personal, social and political spheres, demand constant actions and decisions based on clear convictions, moral ideals and principles. But, if every religion, every philosophy, every moral system is tainted with relativity, merely the product of the strains and stresses, the hopes and intentions of an age, how is decisive action based on independent moral conviction, possible?[16(p57)]

Just as a scientist might compare one group of subjects with another in order to draw conclusions, the scientific historian compared one historical tradition with another and concluded that none of them could claim absolute validity. Why should the ethics of Christianity be more valid than the ethics of Islam? Based on a purely objective, impartial analysis, the historian could only conclude that all moral and ethical values are ultimately relative.

As Western societies became progressively more pluralistic in the twentieth century, the problem of moral relativity became more and more critical. In a society composed of individuals out of diverse religious traditions and ethnic backgrounds, there will necessarily be divergent views on moral values. Since all moral values appear to be historically and culturally conditioned, none of them can claim universal validity. The resulting conflict of moral values leads ultimately to a situation in which any possible course of action can be justified. This is precisely the situation in which we are living today, and it is properly termed "moral nihilism". There *are* no really binding moral values; ergo, "anything goes"!

So where do we go from here? How do we find a new foundation for the moral dimension in society? As we have seen, the development of natural science beginning in the seventeenth century transformed the old Stoic notion of natural law into the laws of nature, and by the late nineteenth century, the methods of scientific inquiry had been applied to the realm of history, thereby demonstrating that all moral values are historically and culturally conditioned and therefore relative. However, there is in this development from the seventeenth to the nineteenth century a deep irony that is often overlooked. Whereas all moral values were robbed of their universal validity, certain constants of nature were discovered that are apparently unchanging and universally valid. One thinks, for instance, of Newton's gravitational constant. The force of gravity acting on a particular body is given by the equation: $F = G \, Mm/r^2$, where M is the mass of the earth, m is the mass of the body, r is the distance from the center of the earth and G is the universal constant 6.67×10^{-11}. The term "constant" indicates that this quantity is independent of time, position, and mass as well as of the nature of the body in question.[19(p28)] Then in the twentieth century, additional universal constants were discovered in connection with the development of the "Special Theory of Relativity" and of Quantum Physics; Albert Einstein proposed that the speed of light "c" is an upper limit with a constant value, and Max Planck discovered experimentally the constant "h", which describes the quantum of action. These, as well as other universal constants in physics, seem to be unchanging and universal, i.e. valid at all times and in all places. In view of this, the question inevitably arises: if there are universal constants in the *realm of nature*, should there not also be universally valid moral values in the *human realm*?

We might attempt to answer this question by referring back to the philosophy of René Descartes and to those who followed in his tradition. In order to preserve the freedom of human beings in the midst of the "Newtonian World Machine", Descartes drew a fundamental distinction between the human mind (*res cogitans*) and physical nature (*res extensa*). Whereas nature is characterized by extension, the human mind consists of thinking. Nature can be measured and quantified, and it obeys the strict laws of causation as formulated by Newton and others. The human mind, on the other hand, has no dimensions and possesses the unique characteristic of freedom. Viewed from this perspective, it would be understandable that scientists have discovered universal constants in nature, but that historians find no universal values in the moral realm. The problem with this explanation is that Descartes' absolute distinction between nature and the mind has proven to be untenable, both from a philosophical as well as from a scientific standpoint. In his scientific theory of evolution, Charles Darwin placed human beings squarely in the midst of nature and argued convincingly that human beings are subject to the same process of evolution as all other species. Philosophically, Descartes' distinction proved to be incoherent because it offered no plausible way to explain the interaction between human beings and nature. If the two realms are really separate, it is not even possible to explain how the physical brain (*res extensa*) is related to the thinking mind (*res cogitans*).

Since an absolute separation between the human realm and the realm of nature is ultimately untenable, we are suggesting in the present work the following procedure: given that it was the scientific investigation of nature beginning in the seventeenth century that eventually led to the relativity of all moral values, and since nature itself has been found to operate according to certain universal constants, and in view of the fact that human beings (body and mind) are in some significant way a part of nature, then the search for legitimate universal values in the moral realm should begin with a reconsideration of the physical world in the hope that our *current* understanding of nature will yield some clues concerning the possibility of universally valid moral values.

Let us start our reconsideration of nature by discussing in somewhat more detail the universal constants. There are four such constants that are generally recognized in physics: Newton's gravitational constant G, Boltzmann's constant k, the speed of light c, and Planck's constant h. For our purposes, it will suffice to discuss the speed of light and its meaning in Einstein's Special Theory of Relativity. Perhaps the easiest way to approach the topic of relativity is to begin with a fairly common situation involving travel on an interstate highway. When I travel by car from my home in The Villages to Gainesville, Florida, I take Interstate Highway 75 North and set the cruise control on 70 miles per hour. Although this is the legal speed limit, there are always drivers on the highway who exceed it to a more or less degree; this "more or less" can easily be estimated by observing the speed with which they overtake and pass me. If they are traveling at a speed of 80 miles per hour, then they pass me with a relative speed of 10 miles per hour. If they are traveling at 90 miles per hour, the relative speed is 20 miles per hour. Such calculations are well known to us and make perfect sense in our everyday lives. Now, let us assume that it is not a car passing me on the interstate, but rather a beam of light. We know that light travels at a speed of 186,000 miles per second. So if I am traveling at a speed of 100 miles per hour, the relative speed of the light beam passing me should be 185,999.99 miles per second. If I were to measure the speed of this light beam, I would, however, not measure 185,999.99, but rather 186,000 miles per second. Admittedly, this difference is so slight that we might well question the accuracy of our results. But if I were traveling in one of NASA's spaceships at a speed of 20,000 miles per hour and were to measure the same beam of light passing the ship, I should detect some significant difference. According to classic physics, the light beam should appear to travel 5.56 miles per second slower than before. Yet, this is not the case. Regardless of how fast I travel, a passing light beam will always be measured at a speed of 186,000 miles per second.

This result is so counterintuitive that no one would have accepted it as correct without the mathematical demonstrations of Albert Einstein. While working in the patent office in Bern, Switzerland, he published in 1905 an article that revolutionized physics. It was entitled: "On the Electrodynamics of Moving Bodies", and it presented the fundamental concepts that have become known as the "Special Theory of Relativity". Einstein's theory postulates that length, time and mass of a body are relative, not absolute. A yardstick going past my spaceship at an extremely high speed will be shorter than when I measured it at rest, and clocks passing by me at high speeds will run slower than at rest. These phenomena are commonly referred to as "length contraction" and "time dilation".

When the "Special Theory of Relativity" became widely known in the United States and Europe, it was generally understood to be a confirmation in the realm of physics of the relativism discovered by the nineteenth-century historicists in the realm of morality and ethics. Just as time, length and the mass of objects are always relative, so too the moral values, the religious views and political ideas are always relative to a particular age. Just as there is no absolute time and space, there are no absolute moral values. To be more specific, since classical physicists like Sir Isaac Newton were wrong about time and space, classical Christian theologians like Augustine and Thomas Aquinas must have been wrong about morality. This everyday understanding of the matter overlooks, however, one enormously significant fact: the speed of light is *absolute*, not *relative*. In fact, it is the invariability of light speed that makes time, length and mass relative. The speed of light is the "fixed point" that does not change. In view of this, it is surprising that historians did not view the "Special Theory of Relativity" as a corrective to their relativism. Historians might well have raised the question as to the possibility of certain "fixed points" in the moral sphere, whereby the meaning of the phrase "fixed point" in this context would certainly require modification.

If we are to overcome the moral relativism of our age, we must attempt to discover something akin to the physical constants in physics, without reverting back to a pre-scientific notion of ahistorical values. We are not proposing that we turn the clock backward to a period before the advent of modern historical studies. Clearly, any attempt to introduce "fixed points" in the sense of timeless, unchanging values would be contradictory and thus untenable. Therefore, it is imperative that we accept as a premise of modern thought that all moral values are the outcome of historical developments in a society and that the notion of *timeless* historical values is self-contradictory. However, the establishment of a timeless basis for morality in a society is quite unnecessary. *The only requirement is that the "fixed points" remain unchanging over a sufficiently long period of time so that they provide moral stability to the society.* Whereas "fixed points" in the realm of physics are numerical constants such as the speed of light, "fixed points" in the moral realm will be concepts–perhaps complex concepts–, and they must be discovered precisely in that being who inhabits this realm: human beings. If we are to locate such "fixed points", we must necessarily concern ourselves with the structure of human existence, or stated more traditionally, with human nature.

Chapter 4

The Self and the Restoration of Natural Law

In his discussion of natural law, Cicero took as his starting point human nature; in *On the Laws*, he writes: "We must explain the nature of law, and that needs to be looked for in human nature..."[7(1.17)] And when he examines human nature, he discovers that the primary characteristic of human beings is reason or right reason. Thus, reason became central to Cicero's understanding of natural law. When we attempt the restoration of natural law more than two thousand years later, we must be aware of the ambiguities in the word "nature" and of the shift in emphasis over the period of two millennia. When Cicero was composing *On the Laws* in the late Roman Republic, he stood on solid ground in proclaiming reason to be the chief characteristic of human beings. After all, Aristotle had defined a human being as the "rational animal" (Latin: *animal rationale*). In his famous work *Concerning the Soul*, Aristotle claimed that every living being has a soul (Greek: *pyche*), whereby he was not employing the word "soul" in a religious, but rather in a purely philosophical sense. When Aristotle wrote about the soul, he was referring to a principle of life that animates the organic world. Plants have the lowest form of soul—the vegetative soul—, which provides the drive to obtain nourishment and to reproduce, in short, the drive of self-preservation. Animals too have this vegetative capacity, but in addition their souls possess sensibility, which grants them the possibility of sense perception. Finally, the soul of a human being possesses not only the vegetative and the sensible faculties, but also the rational, and it is precisely the rational faculty, the capability of rational thought, that distinguishes human beings from all other living creatures.

Thus, the adherents of Aristotle's philosophy defined human beings as the *rational animal* (Greek: *zoon logisticon*, Latin: *animal rationale*).

Cicero adopted this understanding of human nature and felt totally justified in appealing to the rational faculty of humans in discussing natural law. The difference between his world and ours could not be more striking than on this one point. If we were to ask Cicero what it meant for a person to act according to his nature, he would respond by saying that the person would act according to the dictates of right reason. If we were to ask someone today the same question: what does it mean for a person to act according to his nature?, we might well receive the answer that it means "living out" one's desires. Perhaps it is a person's innermost desire to be homosexual. Then, living according to his nature would mean living in a homosexual relationship. Or perhaps it is a person's desire to be sexually promiscuous. Or maybe it is a person's inner desire to be financially successful regardless of the harm inflicted on others. Both Aristotle and Cicero recognized the role of desires in human nature, but for them, most of the desires discussed today belonged to the lowest part of the human soul and were not relevant in attempting to define a life of excellence. With the rise of modern psychology, our understanding of the soul has been inverted so that the lowest part is now given preference in defining individual freedom and fulfillment of life. To state the matter more generally: whatever potentialities a person discovers in himself, that person has the right to actualize these because it is his nature to do so. As we shall see later, this attitude was more or less the position taken by the humanist psychologist Carl R. Rogers. Over a period of time, his humanist program of psychology destroyed multiple families and ruined an entire school of Catholic nuns in Southern California. Admittedly, two thousand years have elapsed between Marcus Cicero and Carl Rogers. Nonetheless, one cannot keep from asking what happened historically to change the situation so dramatically. On the one hand, "living according to nature" means to think and to act rationally in order to attain a *morally virtuous life*. On the other hand, "living according to nature" means to follow without restraint one's *innermost desires*, sexual and otherwise.

What transpired between Cicero and Rogers was a major transition in our understanding of human nature—a transition that is associated with two names: Charles Darwin and Sigmund Freud. To put the matter in the simplest terms: the classical understanding of human nature was undermined by Darwin when he broke down the barrier between animals and human beings, showing that humans have no privileged position in the structure of living creatures. In his publication *The Descent of Man* (1871) he argued that there is no essential difference between human beings and animals. Even the moral sense or conscience of human beings is, according to Darwin, nothing more than the result of the evolutionary process, and if a lower animal were to develop sufficient intellectual powers, it too would have a conscience.[15(p70-72)] Inasmuch as Darwin recognized the rational superiority of human beings, he did not really reject the definition of humans as "rational animal", but in his scientific thinking, the emphasis was placed on "animal", not on "rational". Whereas Cicero defined humans as the *rational* animal, Darwin thought of humans as the rational *animal*.

In the depth psychology of Sigmund Freud, a further development took place that we might call an inversion in the traditional structure of the soul. For Aristotle, the rational faculty of the soul was primary, and one of its chief duties was to keep the vegetative part under control. This understanding of the relationship between reason and desire became a central element of Christian thought in the Middle Ages and found its classical formulation in the theology of Thomas Aquinas. One of the major contributions of Freud was the realization that the vegetative faculty of the soul, i.e. the desires of the lowest part of the psyche, plays a much larger role in the development of the personality and in the daily conduct of the individual than thinkers from Aristotle to Aquinas had recognized. By placing sexuality at the forefront of the psychoanalytic understanding of human nature, Freud was able to demonstrate that the vegetative faculty cannot be controlled as easily as one had thought and that the attempt of the rational part of the soul to control it may lead to severe psychological disorders. In light of this, the traditional structure of human nature appeared untenable, and one of the great challenges that faced Freud was to find a new solution to this problem. Since the desires of the psyche and the rational ability of the psyche are often in conflict, some resolution must be negotiated in the life of the individual. For example, the married executive who *desires* an affair with his secretary knows *rationally* that it may destroy his relationship to family members whom he loves. As a result of his clinical experience with such situations, Freud postulated the "principle of reality" alongside the "pleasure principle", whereby the former was intended to modify the latter in the successful resolution of psychic conflict. In practice, this means that the principle of reality sets definite limits on the immediate and direct gratification of desires. Clearly, the principle of reality plays a similar role in Freud's psychology as the rational faculty in the philosophy of Aristotle, but the differences are more decisive than the similarities. Whereas Aristotle emphasized the rational part of the soul, Freud gave more weight to desires, specifically sexual desires, than any thinker before his time. If we compare Freud's understanding of human nature with that of Cicero and Darwin, we can add a third variation: *rational* animal (Cicero), rational *animal* (Darwin) and *sexual* rational animal (Freud).

Lest I be misunderstood, I would like to assert that I am not finding fault either with Darwin's general theory of evolution or with Freud's basic understanding of the psyche. Their contributions were truly groundbreaking and remain impressive even today. Nevertheless, their innovative ideas paved the way for the sexual revolution of the 1960s as well as for the humanist psychology of Carl Rogers. Neither Darwin nor Freud could have foreseen the direction of thought in the second half of the twentieth century, and both would probably be appalled at the events taking place in our world today.

In light of the difficulties inherent in the concept of human nature, it seems advisable to avoid the word "nature" for the moment and to take our point of departure from a related concept: the structure of *human existence*. In considering the structure of human existence, we will focus on the concept of the *self*. Although the self is a modern concept, it was not totally unknown in antiquity. According to tradition, "Know thyself" was the maxim inscribed at the entrance of the Temple of Apollo at Delphi, northwest of Athens, Greece. Furthermore, "Know thyself" was an admonition that played a central role in the philosophy of Plato, and in the modern era, the attainment of self-knowledge has become the foundation of popular psychology. People read books on psychology in order to understand themselves better; they sometimes join encounter-groups in order to expand their knowledge about themselves; and they also engage in long-term individual therapy in the hope of gaining new insights about themselves. If we spend so much time in our lives trying to know ourselves, the question seems inevitable: what is this *self* that we are trying to understand?

For our purposes, it will suffice to define the self as the *center of experience* in the individual. I experience myself sitting at my desk and writing this book. I experience talking to others and hearing their voice. I see faces in the grocery store and this information enters into my experience as well. I remember something that I read years ago and that too comes into the experience. The self is the center into which information flows and is processed, and this center has an identity in a twofold sense. First of all, the self forms a *unity*. I experience myself as *one* self, not as two.

Even in cases where a split personality develops, each personality experiences itself as a unity. It is precisely the unity of the self that makes coherent experience possible. We receive much more information from the outside world than we can possibly process, but thanks to the unity of the self, we allow some information into our conscious experience and we reject other information. The unity of the self means that we filter out irrelevant information, i.e. information that does not fit the current experience. But the identity of the self is more than its unity at the moment. It is also the *continuity* of this unity over a period of time. The self remains in some sense the same self throughout the life of the person. We don't fall asleep at night as one person and wake up in the morning as somebody else. Each one of us is in some sense the same self over a long period of time. Were this not the case, our legal system would be much more complicated. If the person who committed the crime last month was not the same person who is now on trial for the crime, it is difficult to imagine how our legal system could function. *So the self is the center of experience in the individual, and this center is characterized by self-identity, i.e. by a unity at the moment and by continuity over time.*

Given the importance of self-identity, it is imperative to understand how this self-identity is formed. To be sure, there may be some genetic and endocrinological factors at work, particularly with respect to gender differences. But if we look at the broad picture, we will find that the formation of self-identity is to a large extent a cultural phenomenon. We are born into a particular culture, and aspects of that culture such as language, gender roles and religious views determine the identity of the *self*. Culture is, however, an historical phenomenon; it is affected by historical events and it changes over time. Present day Western cultures are not the same as they were in the sixteenth century, and the historical events of the intervening centuries have had a dramatic impact on the identity of the self. If we want to discover certain "fixed points" in the moral realm, we must determine the fundamental concepts that have emerged over a long period of time and that are now affecting the formation of the self. Let it be noted: *over a long period of time*. The idea that the self is merely a construct of a particular society and that it can be altered relatively easy is nothing more than a fantasy of popular post-modern movements—a fantasy that was promoted by French philosophers such as Michel Foucault and Jacques Derrida. To be sure, self-identity is largely a cultural phenomenon, but the historical waters of culture run very deep and fundamental changes occur very slowly.

In searching for certain "fixed points" that have manifested themselves over a long period of time, we could approach the matter from various perspectives, but it is undeniable that the interaction of science and religion since the beginning of the seventeenth century has been a primary factor. The sixteenth century was expressly religious in tone. We need only remind ourselves that the Protestant reformation as well as the Roman Catholic counter-reformation took place in that century. In contrast, we observe in the seventeenth century the beginnings of modern science in the work of individuals such as Johannes Kepler, Galileo Galilei, Isaac Newton and others, and these early beginnings have led to the world in which we live today, a world dominated by natural science and technology. That the transition from the religiosity of the sixteenth century to the technological age of the twenty-first century has had a definitive impact on human existence, specifically on the identity of the self, should be clear regardless of one's present religious views. Even if one views religion today with indifference, the fact remains that the interaction between science and religion has affected all of us. Therefore, we shall focus on this historical interaction in search of fundamental concepts for understanding the self and its identity.

If we survey the history of the interaction between science and religion since the seventeenth century, we discover that there were certain periods in which the interaction was unusually intense, and these periods can easily be identified with the names: Isaac Newton, Charles Darwin, and Albert Einstein. Before we embark upon this investigation, however, we would like to emphasize once again that we are not proposing specifically theological concepts, although we will be discussing religion from an historical perspective. To be sure, one's religious views may affect the identity of the self in some way, and this holds true whether one's orientation is Christian, Jewish, Muslim, Buddhist or atheistic. If the atheist, for instance, does not experience the divine in any way, this will undoubtedly influence his or her understanding of the self and the formation of self-identity. But we are not concerned in this present study with particular religious views; instead, we are seeking "fixed points" of sufficient generality for society as a whole. Therefore, we have adopted a position on the matter that could be best described in this way: *the self has been analyzed from the standpoint of a humanist living in a culture historically influenced by the Christian tradition.* This methodological point is significant because we are searching for concepts of the self and "fixed points" in the moral realm that are common to all human beings in Western societies.

Let us begin with the physics of Sir Isaac Newton. If we consider the scientific developments of the seventeenth century, Newton certainly stands out as the one who was able to provide a unified theory of motion. Johannes Kepler had made remarkable progress in understanding the movement of the heavenly bodies, and Galileo had made significant advances in grasping the principles involved in the motion of bodies on earth. But it was Newton who developed a theory that could explain the movement of bodies in both regions, the heavenly as well as the terrestrial. In the writings of Kepler, we observe only the beginning of the new scientific concept of force (Latin: *vis*), whereas in Newton's *Principia Mathematica*, the concept emerges as central to the new physics. Admittedly, Newton did not develop his three laws of motion in quite the neat form in which we find them in modern textbooks on physics. He wrote his *opus magnum* not in English, but rather in Latin, and nowhere in this groundbreaking work do we find, for instance, the well-known equation F = ma. In fact, Newton's understanding of force was different from that found in our textbooks. Whereas he defined force in his second law as the change in impulse ($\Delta[m \cdot v]$), our standard textbooks define force as the change of impulse pro unit of time ($\Delta[m \cdot v]/\Delta t$ or simply ma). Furthermore, Newton was not totally clear on the meaning of the word "force", as Max Jammer notes in his detailed analysis of the concept of force in physics. Jammer writes: "it is obvious that the second law of motion was not intended by Newton as a definition of force... Force, for Newton, was a concept given a priori, intuitively, and ultimately in analogy to human muscular force."[20(p124)] The analogy of force to human exertion was not only fundamental to the physics of the seventeenth century, it has remained a connotation of the word up until the present. From our own experience, we know that heavy objects can be moved by sheer force, whether this force is produced directly by the exertion of human muscles or by machines designed by humans. Likewise, if similar forces are applied to human "objects", then they too can be compelled to move in this or that direction. The intensity of the force can be relatively small as in the case of a thrust to the body or devastatingly large as in the explosion of an atomic bomb, but the principle remains the same: we can compel others to comply with our will by the use of force. In order to understand why physical force has become a primary means of dealing with others in interpersonal relationships, we must inquire about Newton's understanding of God.

Contrary to the prevailing opinion about Newton's physics, he never asserted that the physical laws of nature based on his concept of force rendered divine intervention unnecessary. In fact, he considered that the proper motion of the heavenly bodies could not be maintained without occasional adjustment through divine action. In particular, there were two points at which Newton viewed divine action as necessary: to prevent the fixed stars from falling together as a result of gravitational force, and to adjust the deviations of the planets from their normal course, which was also caused by gravitational pull. In his *Opticks* (1704), Newton writes:

> For while comets move in very excentrick orbs in all manner of positions, blind Fate could never make all the planets move one and the same way in orbs concentrick, some inconsiderable irregularities excepted, which may have risen from the mutual actions of comets and planets upon one another, and which will be apt to increase, till this system wants a reformation. Such a wonderful uniformity in the planetary system must be allowed the effect of choice.[14(p261f)]

And further:

> (God is) a powerful ever-living Agent; who being in all places, is more able by his will to move the bodies within his boundless uniform sensorium, and thereby to form and reform the parts of the universe, than we are by our will to move the parts of our own bodies.[14(p262)]

When the system of the planets requires a "reformation", i.e. a correction, the will of God moves the heavenly bodies into their proper positions. So alongside the laws of nature, Newton saw the necessity of divine causation in order to preserve the harmony of the universe. When he writes about "the effect of (God's) choice", it is clear that he understands God as the *cause* and the alteration in the movement of the planetary system as the *effect*. But how could God cause such changes in the movement of the planets? In Newton's unified view, the entire universe was thought to be moved by physical forces. Since nothing in this mechanical world could take place that was not caused by some physical force, it was also necessary to conceive of God's interaction with the world in this manner. Thus, Newton concluded that God causes the alteration of the movement of the planets through the exercise of force. For this reason, Newton frequently referred to God as the "*Pantokrator*", the Greek word for the "Almighty". To be sure, Christian theologians before Newton had thought of God as the "Almighty" (Latin: *omnipotent*), but they had understood the attribution to mean all-powerful. Furthermore, during the Protestant reformation of the sixteenth century, Martin Luther had emphasized repeatedly that God's omnipotence is expressed primarily in the Word of God, i.e. in language. According to Luther, it is in language that the power of God is manifested.

With the transition from the sixteenth to the seventeenth century, we witness a remarkable change. Whereas the theological tradition had always spoken of God's omnipotence, meaning God's attribute of being *all-powerful*, the mechanical world of physical forces led to the notion of God's attribute of being *all-forceful*. With this, the power of God in the medium of language was concealed, and this eclipse of divine power eventually extended into all areas of society where force became the only means of dealing with relationships, whether these relationships were to nature or to other human beings. Just as Newton interpreted God in terms of force, we have come to understand the self in terms of force, and we are convinced that a strong self-identity is one that is capable of exerting force. So today, the hallmark of our relationship to nature is force; we no longer view nature with a sense of wonder and reverence, but rather we force nature to obey our will. Likewise, the standard of our relationship to other persons has become force, and conflict resolution has become a contest of strength, i.e. of brute force. In this context, power has totally lost its meaning. Power has much more in common with love and respect than it does with force and violence. Power draws people into agreement; force coerces them into obedience.

Our analysis of force in physics and its implications for an understanding of the self should not be interpreted as a complete rejection of force in the human realm. We are not suggesting that force is never necessary, but in our view force should only be employed when power has clearly failed. That is to say, in human relationships, whether on an individual, a national or an international level, the use of force is always a tacit admission of failure. Had we been powerful enough, the force would have been unnecessary. The insight that excessive force is a sign of failure begins to disclose the *polarity between force and power* that is an essential part of natural law. The law of nature requires that this polarity be balanced in the structure of the self. Such a balance between force and power in the self would be manifested outwardly in the interplay between the power of language and the necessity of limited force. Obviously, such a balance is not a "given" in life. It must be attained.

Classical physics reached its final form in the eighteenth century in the work of Leonhard Euler and Joseph Louis Lagrange. In spite of the groundbreaking work of Sir Isaac Newton, his *Principia Mathematica* exhibited significant shortcomings that needed to be remedied. It is not unimportant to note that the full title of Newton's opus magnum read: *Philosophiae Naturalis Principia Mathematica*, i.e. *The Mathematical Principles of Natural Philosophy*. Although we take it for granted that physics is a natural *science*, Newton viewed it as a part of natural *philosophy*, and therefore, his work contained metaphysical and theological ideas that were not really consistent with the development of modern science. During the eighteenth century, the Swiss physicist and mathematician Leonhard Euler and the French physicist Joseph Louis Lagrange succeeded in eliminating

Newton's philosophical and theological ideas from physics, thus placing physics on a purely scientific footing. By the early nineteenth century, the interest in natural philosophy had shifted to a great extent from the inorganic to the organic realm. The so-called "Newtonian World Machine" provided a picture of a world in which all interactions were governed by physical forces that could be mathematically quantified and expressed in scientific equations such as F=ma. But significantly, the "Newtonian World Machine" with its closed nexus of cause and effect applied only to the *inorganic* realm; classical physics could not explain the phenomenon of *life*. Thus, the idea of life retained much of its old religious and philosophical significance, that is, until Charles Darwin developed his theory of evolution. Just as Sir Isaac Newton had developed a new understanding of the inorganic world, Darwin provided a new understanding of the organic world.

Prior to Darwin's work, the organic world was thought to be hierarchically structured with humankind as the pinnacle. The notion of humankind as the top of the pyramid was supported biblically by the creation narrative in Genesis as well as by certain other passages such as Psalm 8, where we read: "Yet thou hast made him little less than God, and dost crown him with glory and honor. Thou hast given him dominion over the works of thy hands: thou hast put all things under his feet." Additionally, the superiority of humans was supported philosophically by the writings of Aristotle, especially his work on psychology entitled *Concerning the Soul*. As we have seen, only human beings have the capacity of reason, and therefore Aristotle placed human beings at the top of the pyramid as the "rational animal". Finally, the hierarchy of the organic world descending from humans to animals and then to plants was considered to be stable and unchanging, and this idea of the constancy of the species was thoroughly consistent with the Newtonian mechanical universe, which was also unchanging.

The fact that the laws of Newton did not apply to the organic world encouraged theologians of the Anglican Church to focus on life as evidence of the existence of God. Foremost among these Anglican theologians was William Paley (born 1743) who published in 1802 his classic work *Natural Theology or Evidences of the Existence and Attributes of the Deity*. This book became a standard textbook in Christ's College in Cambridge where Charles Darwin studied theology, and when Darwin took his theological exams in 1831, he was tested on the theology of William Paley. So if we want to understand how Darwin in his early years understood God in relation to life, we have to read Paley's theology, where we find the classic argument for the existence of God: the Watchmaker. Paley writes:

In crossing a heath, suppose I pitched my foot against a *stone*, and were asked how the stone came to be there, I might possibly answer, that for any thing I knew to the contrary, it had lain there forever; nor would it perhaps be very easy to shew the absurdity of this answer. But suppose I had found a *watch* upon the ground, and it should be enquired how the watch happened to be in that place, I should hardly think of the answer which I had before given, that, for any thing I knew, the watch might have always been there. Yet, why should not this answer serve for the watch, as well as for the stone? Why is it not as admissible in the second case, as in the first? For this reason, and for no other, viz. that, when we come to inspect the watch, we perceive (what we could not discover in the stone) that its several parts are framed and put together for a purpose...This mechanism being observed (it requires indeed an examination of the instrument, and perhaps some previous knowledge of the subject, to perceive and understand it; but being once, as we have said, observed and understood,) the inference, we think, is inevitable; that the watch must have had a maker; that there must have existed, at some time and at some place or other, an artificer or artificers who formed it for the purpose, which we find it actually to answer; who comprehended its construction, and designed its use.[21(p7f)]

Applying the analogy of the watch and the watchmaker to the organic world, Paley presents an argument for the existence of God based on design. Because we observe order and design in the world, particularly in the organic world, we can reasonably infer that there was a being who designed it. Where there's a watch, there must be a watchmaker; where there's design in nature, there must have been a designer, that is, a creator. Consider, for example, the birds in a particular area. We note that the length of their beaks is well suited to the area in which they live; such design and hence the existence of a designer are, according to Paley, irrefutable. Yet, Darwin did refute it and he did it very convincingly.

Without going into detail, we can say that the two main ideas of Darwin's theory are *variation* and *natural selection*. As an illustration, consider a particular species of birds. Individual birds in one generation reproduce birds in the next generation that are not exact copies of their parents. That is, certain variations occur in the next generation—say, for instance, the length of the beak— that help these birds adapt to their surroundings and survive. If birds with shorter beaks miss out and fail to find food, they will not reproduce and leave descendants. The birds with longer beaks will be able to survive and reproduce so that the third generation will also have longer beaks. Note that the competition is within the same species. The individuals of the species are competing in the same area for the same food and for a mate of the same species in order to reproduce. Just as a cell phone company doesn't compete with a fast food company, birds don't compete with elephants. Over a long period of time, the process of natural selection based on the competitive advantage of certain variations produces new species.

That Darwin's theory of evolution hit the nerve of the Anglican Church was apparent shortly after the publication of *On the Origin of Species* in 1859 and was epitomized in the famous debate between Thomas Huxley and Bishop Samuel Wilberforce at the University of Oxford in 1860. As we have seen, the chief argument for the existence of God in the Anglican Church was the argument from design. The order and design of the organic world point to a creator. Darwin agrees that there is a certain order in the organic world, but from this fact, he draws a totally different conclusion. He says in effect: "Yes, we see order in the universe. The birds in this area have nice long beaks so that they can obtain the necessary food for their survival. But the reason that we observe these birds with nice long beaks is because all of the short beaked birds died out! It's not because a supreme Being designed it this way. It's because only those individuals survive that fit their environment."

There we have a perfectly reasonable scientific explanation for the orderliness of nature, leaving us unsure whether we are observing any real design or just plain biological accident. Furthermore, if the species that we observe today are really just the outcome of a long series of biological accidents, how can we seriously talk about the dignity of human beings? In one fell swoop, Darwin dismantled two of the most important ideas of the Anglican Church: the design argument for the existence of God and the dignity of humankind as the pinnacle of creation. There were details of Darwin's theory of evolution that required modification, and the mechanism by which the variations occurred was not known until the discovery of DNA in 1953. Nevertheless, the substance of his theory was correct and has had a tremendous impact on the self-understanding of human beings. Darwin's theory leads to two inescapable conclusions. Firstly, there is no qualitative difference between humans and lower animals. Secondly, there is no ultimate purpose in the life process; that is, life is not directed toward any goal (*telos*).

What distinguishes Darwin's understanding of life from all previous conceptions, whether in the Greek philosophical tradition or in Christian theology, is the reduction of the phenomenon of life to specific biological and chemical processes. The idea of an animating principle in organic forms—an *élan vital*—, has been completely eliminated. In this reductionistic view, the life of an individual is nothing more than a complex biochemical process and is, in principle, not to be elevated above the life of a fruit fly. After the decoding of the human genome and that of the fruit fly, there were headlines in all leading science publications about the remarkable similarity of the two. Nevertheless, there remains in our language and in our everyday thought reflections of "something more" in life than just these processes. When we say, for instance: "There was no life in her dancing", we do not mean that all biochemical processes had ceased to function; we mean instead that her dancing lacked spirit, it lacked animation. And when we attend a funeral and someone says: "He had in many ways a tragic life", we do not understand the statement as a reference to his biochemical processes. Tragedy has to do with the frustrated aspirations of the human spirit, not with biochemical processes. The insight that life can be tragic, that life can fail or succeed, begins to disclose the *polarity of life and the spirit* that is essential to natural law.

The empiricist may object to the introduction of the word "spirit" in a secular context, but the objection that only empirical data can be considered valid fails from the outset. Perhaps the empiricist's view had some credibility in the seventeenth century when physics was investigating large objects, but in the world of quantum physics, it makes no sense at all. Furthermore, one should note that we are not introducing the notion of "spirit" in reference to a divine being. The word "spirit" in Hebrew (*ruah*), for instance, originally meant "breath", "wind" or "spirit" in the sense of animation, and it is precisely in this sense that we understand it. In short, "spirit" means in the context of the present investigation the "human spirit", not the "Holy Spirit". The human spirit is not necessarily religious, but it does have an intangible quality. It is the "something more" that is added to the biochemical processes that enables a life to be successful or tragic. Just as natural law is defined by the polarity of force and power, it is also defined by the polarity of life and spirit.

We turn now to the twentieth century, in which another scientific revolution took place. In the last chapter, we discussed Einstein's "Special Theory of Relativity" in connection with the problem of relativism in general. We now take up this topic again in order to see how some aspects of the theory have affected our understanding of the self. That Einstein's theory brought about a genuine revolution of scientific thought can easily be seen by considering the attitudes of the scientific community at the turn of the twentieth century. In 1903, the American physicist Albert Abraham Michelson published a work entitled *Light Waves and Their Uses*, in which he brought the widespread optimism to expression that theoretical physics had already been worked out in completion and that the only remaining tasks for the future would be the refinement of the present theories. He wrote:

> What would be the use of such extreme refinement in the science of measurement? Very briefly and in general terms the answer would be that in this direction the greater part of all future discovery must lie. The more important fundamental laws and facts of physical science have all been discovered, and these are now so firmly established that the possibility of their ever being supplanted in consequence of new discoveries is exceedingly remote.[22(p23f)]

Two years later, Albert Einstein published his "Special Theory of Relativity", in which he demonstrated that classical physics was only a special case of a more comprehensive theory of the relativity of time, space and mass. Of particular interest to us is the concept of time.

Although Einstein's original theory was based primarily on mathematical deductions, not on empirical data, other scientists have confirmed the correctness of his theory by designing and performing the necessary experiments. Particularly interesting in this regard is the verification of the time dilation phenomenon. In 1971, Joseph Hafele, a physicist, and Richard Keating, an astronomer, performed an experiment using four cesium-beam atomic clocks of extremely high accuracy. They mounted the four clocks in commercial airliners and flew twice around the world, first eastward, then westward. Upon returning, they compared these clocks with others that had remained at the US Naval Observatory, and the results confirmed beyond all doubt the validity of Einstein's theory. If we take the clocks at the Naval Observatory to be the frame of reference at rest, then the clocks moving eastward in the direction of the earth's rotation have a greater velocity than the ones at rest, whereas the clocks moving westward have a lower velocity than the ones at rest. According to the "Special Theory of Relativity", the clocks moving eastward should run slower, while the ones moving westward should run faster. The comparison of the clocks at the end of the experiment confirmed within tolerable limits the predicted loss and gain of time. In short, faster moving clocks run slowly; time slows down.

Just as fast moving clocks run slower, fast moving yardsticks get shorter, and this correlation of time dilation and length contradiction led to a new understanding of the world in which we live. In classical physics, space was thought to have three dimensions and time to have one dimension. So any event could be specified by giving its three spatial coordinates and the time at which it occurred. In the "Special Theory of Relativity", space and time were combined into a single four-dimensional space-time continuum. The result of this radical change was to rob time of its independent status over against space, and to alter the way in which we think about time.

In order to grasp the full significance of this change, we must consider it against the background of two different under-standings of time, both of which date back to classical Greek philosophy. Let us begin with an everyday situation. If you ask someone the question: "What time is it?", you will undoubtedly receive an answer involving numbers, for instance: "It's 9:30 p.m." Such an answer is so common in our everyday lives that we rarely reflect upon the connection between *time* and *numbers*. Every household has at least one clock, and many individuals wear a wrist watch daily. All such devises are provided with numbers so that we can determine the correct time. If we have only two hours to perform a certain task, we need to know how much time has elapsed since we began. From this, we can draw a further conclusion. Time not only has something to do with *numbers,* time is *measurable*. Then measuring is one of the primary functions of numbers. If we adopt our "clock time" as funda-mental, we arrive at a linear view of time as a series of points, each of which follows the one before it and all of which can be counted. Applying this view of time to the life of a human being, life seems to be a one-way street which leads from birth to death, with no possibility of turning back and with no possibility of continuing indefinitely.

The other understanding of time stemming from ancient philosophy lacks numbers altogether and cannot be quantified. Trying to think about time without numbers will strike us at first as an odd endeavor because the linear view of time as a series of points was the basis of classical physics in the seventeenth and eighteenth centuries and is still primary today in the natural sciences. Nevertheless, the grammatical structure of our language points us immediately in a different direction by distin-guishing three modes of time: past, present and future. Events that have already occurred belong to the past; events that are taking place now belong to the present; and events that have not yet occurred belong to the future. It is interesting to note that we can discuss these modes of time without any reference to numbers. Still, it may seem at first glance that the modes of times represent a series like our clock time, albeit a series that begins with past and ends with future. The apparent similarity with clock time is, however, only an illusion, and as soon as we introduce the other tenses, namely present perfect, past perfect and future perfect, we realize that the modes of times describe events and their relevance, not points in a series. Both the past tense and the present perfect tense refer to a completed event, but they refer to it differently. The present perfect tense indicates relevance for the present that is not expressed in the past tense. "I have lived here for three years" does not have the same meaning as "I lived here for three years." Or consider the present tense. "He eats cereal for breakfast" does not mean that he did this at *one* point in a series, but rather that he does it habitually. The attempt to correlate the modes of time with points in a series is frustrated at every turn for the following reason. *Time as a series of points has an essential connection with numbers, whereas time as a description of events is inherently related to language.* Just as the words in a sentence hang together and convey a meaning, the modes of time are interrelated and enable unified experiences. The interrelatedness of past, present and future is apparent in the experience of promise and fulfillment; what was promised in the past and anticipated in the future is fulfilled in the present. Past, present and future are not three *points* in a series, but a *unified experience*. If we look for similes to describe this difference, we could say that clock time is like a *string of beads*, whereas modal time is like a *woven cloth*.

Even in the early days of physics as represented in the work of Galileo and Newton, *clock time* began to take precedence over *modal time*. Physics is based on mathematical calculations and requires numbers. Already in the representation of time as a series of points that can be counted, a subtle spatialization of time took place that tended to separate the self from the more fundamental experience of past, present and future. But it was in the "Special Theory of Relativity" that this spatialization of time reached its completion through the integration of the time dimension into a four-dimensional space-time continuum—a continuum in which measurable time is analogous to space and lacks any relationship to modal time. In our technological age, the fundamental experience of unified time has been obscured by the predominance of clock time. What we experience day after day is time as a series of points and our lives as a one-way street. Without the experience of unified time, we struggle to hold time together. We try to stabilize the self through the consumption of goods. We seek religious views that are absolute, and we apply external ethical standards that are no longer grounded in our own experience of time. In short, having lost the experience of unified time, we struggle to establish the unity and continuity of the self, both of which are constitutive for self-identity. Should the bond between clock time and modal time ever be totally severed, we would cease to be human beings, but the situation today is so extreme that we can appropriately say that we are suffering under the burden of clock time and are finding it increasingly difficult to establish self-identity.

The insight that clock time is inadequate for the well-being of humans and that the unified experience of past, present and future is more fundamental begins to disclose the *polarity of time and eternity* that is essential to natural law. For in the philosophical tradition, the word "eternity" referred to the perfect unity of past, present and future in the experience of the individual. In introducing the word "eternity", we must be careful to distinguish it from the notion of "everlasting". In everyday parlance, eternity is often considered to be the state of the individual *after* death, and for this reason, eternity is thought to be synonymous with *afterlife*. This usage of the word "eternity" is, however, unsatisfactory because it indicates a further point in the series. It is as if the life of the person took place in time from point A to point B, and then afterlife began at point C and continued forever in an endless series. But afterlife in this sense is *everlasting*, not *eternal*. The word "eternity" has in the philosophical as well as in the theological tradition a different meaning, and this meaning can only be grasped if we move beyond the clock time that is so predominant in our society.

Plato once described time as the "moving image of eternity", whereby he meant that time and eternity were not to be separated as though eternity were timeless.[23(37d5)] Time and eternity belong together fundamentally, and in some way, time reflects eternity: It is the moving image of eternity. For our purposes, it suffices to say that eternity is the perfection or completion of time so that time occurs in its purity as an integrated whole. In the experience of eternity *in* time, everything has its place, nothing is lost. These are elevated moments of life, moments of intense joy, in which we experience a *completion* of time, whereby past and future seem to coalesce in the present. This experience of the perfection of time without a hint of loss, untainted by melancholy, is the experience of *eternity* in time. Since the unified experience of time is essential for establishing self-identity, i.e. the unity and continuity of the self, the polarity of time and eternity belongs essentially to natural law.

Let us summarize the results of our investigation to this point. By examining the history of the interaction of natural science and religion, as exemplified in the works of Sir Isaac Newton, Charles Darwin and Albert Einstein, we have arrived at certain "fixed points" in the moral realm, which are analogous to the universal constants in physics. At first, it appeared that the "fixed points" were the simple concepts: force, life and time, but further consideration of the matter led to the insight that each of these simple concepts is one side of a polarity. If we visualize the simple concepts as the North Pole, then we can consider that each of them has a South Pole, which is essentially related to it. In the course of our analysis, it turned out that the polarities are: *force-power, life-spirit and time-eternity*. These polarities can be designated most properly as the "fixed points" in the moral realm. They constitute the most fundamental layer of natural law (*lex naturalis*) and are essential for forming the *identity* of the self.

As we have seen, the identity of the self involves two elements. Firstly, the self forms a *unity*. Each one of us experiences him- or herself as *one* self, not as two, and it is precisely the unity of the self that makes coherent experience possible. We receive much more information from the outside world than we can possibly process, and in order to preserve the unity of the self, we allow some information into our conscious experience and reject other information. In view of this, the question naturally arises as to the individual differences among human beings. Why is it that Mr Jones allows different information into his conscious experience than Mrs Smith? To be sure, past experiences play a significant role, but past experiences themselves require in turn an explanation. If we push the question of individual differences to the limit, we will find that the constitution of the polarities is fundamental.

The way in which force and power, for instance, are related in the self will be determinative for the kind of information that can be unified in the conscious experience of the individual and consequently also for the behavior of the individual. Remember that the physical world is the medium of force, whereas language is the medium of power. If force and power are out of balance in the identity of the self, the individual will be much more prone to the exercise of force or even to acts of violence than the circumstances would seem to warrant. The inability to carry on dialogue with others and the tendency to violence are clear signs of a self-identity in which the polarity of force and power is seriously out of balance. A similar analysis can be applied to the polarity of life and spirit. If this polarity is seriously out of balance, the spirit will be obscured, and life will appear as a purely biological matter. The individual will place an inordinate emphasis on physical survival to the exclusion of any other considerations, and the self-identity of the individual will be determined by his physical surroundings, including the person's body. The undue preoccupation of a person with his body is a clear sign of a self-identity formed by the distorted polarity of life and spirit. That this condition is widespread in Western societies requires little verification; whether we consider the exaggerated worry of individuals about their health, the neurotic preoccupation with physical beauty or the libertarian insistence of sexual experience in any and every form, we cannot deny the unbalanced concern for the physical, i.e. for life as a biological process. Finally, the polarity of time and eternity can be unbalanced to the extent that eternity is totally obscured, leaving the self, as it were, set adrift in time. Without the experience of the eternal *in* time, self-identity becomes difficult to establish because there is no apparent continuity of the self over time. The lack of stability in the self makes it virtually impossible to find an Archimedes' point for moral judgment. Furthermore, since time becomes the only realm in which the life of the individual unfolds, the individual develops unrealistic expectations of time; the self rushes from one experience to another in a futile attempt to experience as much as possible in the short span of time allotted to a human being. In this condition, time reveals its character as demand, and the self suffers under the pressure of time.

Although we have analyzed the three polarities separately, it should be emphasized that they are interrelated in forming the self-identity of the individual. An example should make this clear. Let us imagine an individual whose identity has been formed by an extreme imbalance of all three polarities. Since the polarity of time and eternity is obscured, the individual will experience only time and will, therefore, feel the pressure of time to "make the most" of the time allotted to him. For this person, that which does not happen in time is lost forever. Since the polarity of life and spirit is out of balance, the entire focus of the individual will be on his biological life, and should the individual be dissatisfied with his sexual life, the pressure of time will push the individual to seek some kind of change. At this point, one could imagine that the individual would seek counseling in order to effect some change in the self-identity, but given the imbalance in the polarity of force and power, a solution in the medium of language is blocked since, as we have learned, language is the medium of power, not force. If a change is to be effected, it must be accomplished through force, and as we have learned, the medium of force is the physical world. In this arena, technology reigns, and the medical profession has provided the necessary tools for whatever change one desires.

From the foregoing, it is abundantly clear that an actual balance of the polarities is never automatically given in the self. There is a myriad of ways in which the self can be structured, i.e. in which the polarities can be realized, but natural law urges us to find some way of *balancing* them in forming our self-identity. According to natural law, there is a healthy balance between force and power, time and eternity, life and spirit, and in striving toward this balance, the individual may indeed attain a *life of excellence*. The punishment for violation of the natural law is not the thunder and lightning of divine retribution, but rather self-estrangement. In violating the natural law, we violate ourselves and separate our actual selves from our true selves. The unbalanced self, separated from power, spirit and eternity, is its own punishment.

In the preceding discussion, the impression may have arisen that we are analyzing the self as if it were an isolated entity in a laboratory test tube. Obviously, no such self has ever existed. The self is always a self in *relation* to a world, whether that world is the nurturing mother of the newborn or the political world of the adult diplomat. From this, it should be clear that the natural law has both an *individual* and a *societal* dimension. The emphasis can be either on the centered self as it establishes its own identity or on the societal self as it expresses itself in the world, but in both cases the self is embedded in relationships.

Chapter 5

Natural Law in Society

In establishing its identity, the self struggles to find a balance between force and power, time and eternity, life and spirit. In relating to society, the self discovers that these polarities of natural law become processes: *self-knowledge, self-actualization and the transformation of relationships*. Let us begin with the process of self-knowledge.

Self-knowledge cannot be attained if the self is cut off from all relationships. The idea of an individual living totally alone from birth and attaining thereby a profound understanding of him- or herself is quite simply an illusion. Without the network of relationships, which we call a society, the isolated individual would not even acquire language, and without language, self-knowledge is impossible. The attainment of self-knowledge requires the presence of the *Other* in the immediate world of the self. For the newborn infant, the first and primary Other is the mother; at some point in its development, the infant distinguishes between itself and the mother. Suddenly, the self perceives the mother as not-self, as the Other in the relationship, and reflected in the Other, the self acquires knowledge of its own limits and boundaries, not just the boundaries and limits of its physical body, but also of its capabilities. The infant cries and the mother rushes to its aid; the self expresses itself and the Other responds. Or the infant cries too much, and the mother leaves it in the crib; the self expresses itself again, but this time the Other doesn't respond. Here we see the rudimentary beginnings of self-knowledge. But the attainment of self-knowledge in the truest sense does not really begin until the child acquires linguistic skills. With the acquisition of language, the child enters a new stage of consciousness in which it can communicate a much wider range of feelings and ideas, likes and dislikes with the Other. The child learns the meaning of the word "no" and becomes aware of new boundaries outside of itself. As new physical as well as psychological boundaries are set in place, the self takes on contours and learns progressively more about itself.

Self-knowledge is a process that continues throughout the life of an individual. Only through the presence of the Other can the adult self recognize its own tendency to hybris. Only through the presence of the Other does the self learn about its own capabilities, both positive and negative. As we have indicated, the child usually acquires basic self-knowledge through interaction with his/her parents. But if the development of the self takes an abnormal course in childhood, the adult self may require the somewhat artificial setting of psychotherapy for the attainment of self-knowledge, whereby the therapist serves as the Other in order to correct the maladjustment of the individual. Yet, even in cases of optimal childhood development, the process of attaining self-knowledge continues throughout the life of the individual. In a marriage relationship, for instance, one partner serves as the Other for the other partner in the continual process of attaining self-knowledge. Through dialogue with each other, through confrontation and compromise, the self learns step by step more about itself.

Many years ago, I had a conversation with a man at a Kiwanis Club meeting who told me that he and his wife had never had an argument. According to him, they were always in agreement on important issues. Assuming that he was telling me the truth, he described unwittingly a most unfortunate situation. A marriage relationship in which there is never any disagreement or confrontation is one in which neither partner ever has the opportunity to expand his or her self-knowledge. Traditionally, it was thought that the cognitive and affective differences between men and women were beneficial to both the husband and the wife in a marriage relationship. Whether same-sex relationships will provide the same benefits for the attainment of self-knowledge remains to be seen. Be that as it may, the major problem for the attainment of self-knowledge in Western societies lies in another area.

It is generally accepted today that we have moved from the industrial age to the information age, but the impact of this transition is not yet well understood. What we are discovering at the moment is this: with the transition from the industrial to the information age, the Other is becoming *virtual*; that is, we are depending more and more on electronic information provided through media such as television, video games, iPhones etc. for the process of attaining self-knowledge. But the *virtual* Other is by definition not real and cannot really assist us in attaining self-knowledge. Consider the relation between a person and a computer. There is still talk in some circles about the possibility of constructing a computer that has the characteristics of a human being. We know that computers can make very complicated computations much faster and much more accurately than humans, but we have not yet come to the point where we feel comfortable claiming that there is an equivalence between computers and humans. Furthermore, it is not totally clear what attributes the computer must have in order to qualify as human. In any case, the possibility of building a "human-like" computer has raised numerous social and ethical concerns in the general public as well as in the scientific community. In his book *Payback* (2009), Frank Schirrmacher, one of the editors of the German newspaper *Frankfurter Allgemeinen Zeitung*, discusses this matter and argues that we are thinking about the problem in the wrong way. According to him, the real danger is not that we construct a computer capable of thinking and behaving like a human being, but rather that human beings become more and more like computers in their thinking and behaving. Our ever-increasing reliance on the virtual Other is changing our thought patterns, our social behavior and our understanding of ourselves.

In general, the shift from the *real* Other to the *virtual* Other is resulting in an unprecedented preoccupation with entertainment and a concomitant superficiality of self-knowledge. Manuel Castells, author of *The Rise of the Network Society* (1996), refers to the media scholar Neil Postman, who has criticized in particular television for its tendency to convert every topic into entertainment. Castells writes:

> (Neil Postman) considers that television represents an historical rupture with the typographic mind. While print favors systematic exposition, TV is best suited to casual conversation. To make this distinction sharply, in his own words: "Typography has the strongest possible bias towards exposition: a sophisticated ability to think conceptually, deductively and sequentially; a high valuation of reason and order; an abhorrence of contradiction; a large capacity for detachment and objectivity; and a tolerance for delayed response." While for television, "entertainment is the supra-ideology of all discourse on television. No matter what is depicted or from what point of view, the overarching presumption is that it is there for our amusement and pleasure."[24(p360f)]

The emphasis on "amusement and pleasure" that is offered by the new virtual Other cannot expand our self-knowledge in depth. Even so-called serious television presentations such as the documentaries of the Public Broadcasting Service are designed to be entertaining and do not challenge the individual to self-examination in the same way that another human being does.

Moving from television to the internet, we find that the development of virtual communities on the internet has added a new dimension to the problem of superficiality. Castells comments:

> A key distinction in the analysis of sociability is that between weak ties and strong ties. The Net is particularly suited to the

development of multiple weak ties. Weak ties are useful in providing information and opening up opportunities at a low cost. The advantage of the Net is that it allows the forging of weak ties with strangers, in an egalitarian pattern of interaction where social characteristics are less influential in framing, or even blocking, communication.[24(p388)]

Castells acknowledges the advantages of the internet with regard to the formation of *weak* relationships, but weak relationships such as those formed at annual neighborhood socials are not adequate for the attainment of self-knowledge. To be sure, weak virtual relationships can be quickly established, but they can be just as quickly terminated—with a mouse click. Acquiring self-knowledge is a progress that requires time, patience and endurance; it requires delving into ourselves in the process of relating to the Other which sets limits on us, challenges us, encourages us and in so doing provides us with a mirror in which we can learn about ourselves.

The *process of self-actualization* begins already with the individual's knowledge of innate capabilities and intrinsic limitations, but it unfolds progressively in a network of relationships in society that extend far beyond the Other of self-knowledge. Such self-actualization takes place quite normally in children as they mature. Whereas the acquisition of language is the pre-condition for attaining self-knowledge, the social milieu of the classroom or some comparable group can be considered essential for the process of self-actualization. In relating to the teachers and to the other pupils, the young child develops and actualizes his or her potentialities. Like the process of self-knowledge, the process of self-actualization continues throughout the lives of individuals as they establish social relationships. In social clubs and religious organizations, the individual has the opportunity to develop new aspects of the self. Since the 1960s, many adults have even found it helpful to participate in special groups designed for the specific purpose of self-actualization. Carl Rogers, one of the co-founders of the "Association for Humanistic Psychology" in the late 1950s, termed such specifically designed settings "encounter groups", and throughout his career, he promoted the idea that self-actualization always occurs in a network of social relationships.

Just as natural law obligates us to strive toward self-knowledge, it also places upon us the obligation to develop the innate potentialities that we possess. We are to become the very best human beings that we are capable of becoming. However, the best that *I* can become is not to be confused with the best of *all* human beings. Developing our potentialities is not a contest to determine who is the best, and therefore a comparison of our progress with others is often misleading. If I have a natural talent for music and an apparent gift of dexterity on the piano, the natural law requires me to develop this talent. Yet, a comparison of myself with Ludwig von Beethoven is not only senseless, but probably counterproductive. Becoming another Beethoven is not the measure of my success; success in fulfilling the natural law consists in becoming the very best that *I* am capable of becoming.

Unfortunately, Western cultures encourage every one of us daily to compare ourselves with others who supposedly represent the ideal. Fashion magazines present models who are supposed to be the ideal for every woman, and advertisements bombard men with the ideal picture of male strength and virility. In most cases, the aim of such comparisons is the promotion of consumerism, and the message is remarkably simple: "Buy this product and you will come closer to the ideal!" Yielding to the influence of advertising, we tend to channel our efforts of self-actualization into the fruitless attempt to imitate others. The result of this mania is clear. Instead of developing our real potentialities, we frustrate ourselves by trying to imitate others who have potentialities different than ours. If I have a talent to write books, why should I frustrate myself trying to be the best quarterback on a football team? As a youth, I actually tried this, and the price that I paid for it was a broken knee and a chipped tooth. How helpful it would have been, if someone had told me that all of us don't have the same talents! Similarly, every young girl is not destined to be the "beauty queen" of her school. So why do we exalt physical beauty as the most important quality that a young girl can possess? Success lies not in a *strained imitation* of others, but rather in the *authentic actualization* of ourselves—that is, in the actualization of those innate potentialities, which each and every one of us possesses.

Thus far, we have discussed potentialities as though all of them were necessarily positive. Indeed, the humanistic psychology of Carl Rogers was based on the view that the underlying actualizing tendency in human beings is always positive and constructive, i.e. that "the core of man's nature is essentially positive".[25(p73)] Early in his career, Rogers himself recognized that this was a bold hypothesis, but in the course of time, he became convinced that it had been confirmed by his experience as a therapist. However, Abraham Maslow was critical of Rogers' position on human nature and maintained that the methods of humanistic psychology could have very negative consequences if one overlooked the possibility of destructive potentialities in the self. Even some of Rogers' staunch supporters such as William Coulson recognized eventually that the methods were unleashing potentialities of the self that were destroying individuals as well as the groups in which they participated. Although Coulson was for many years a researcher at Rogers' Western Behavioral Sciences Institute in La Jolla, California, in the early 1970s he began to question the validity of humanistic psychology, and after observing the devastating effects of Rogers' methods on the Sisters of the Immaculate Heart of Mary in California, he repudiated the movement and tried to repair the damage that they had done. In essence, he came to agree with

Maslow. Without clear criteria for distinguishing between constructive and destructive potentialities, the encounter groups that promote self-actualization can be very dangerous. Both performing music and committing murder are potentialities of the self that can be actualized. Being a faithful and caring husband is a potentiality of self, but abandoning one's wife in order to discover new aspects of one's own sexuality is also a potentiality of the self. So in pursuing self-actualization, we need some criteria for distinguishing between constructive and destructive potentialities. In general, we can say that constructive potentialities are those which enhance not only the individual self, but also the persons who compose the nearer and wider social network of the self. That is to say, self-actualization ceases to be authentic if it becomes self-centered and destructive of its social context.

The philosophers of antiquity were quite clear in maintaining that humans are essentially social-political beings. We are human beings inasmuch as we participate in a society, and successful participation in a society precludes extreme self-centeredness. In his work *The Republic*, Plato compares the *civic* life to the *psychic* and draws some very interesting parallels. If the parts of the psyche are in conflict with each other, the entire psychic life of the individual is an unhappy one. Allowing free rein to the sensual impulses of the psyche produces a disharmony with the individual's awareness of higher values; passion comes into conflict with reason. Passions of the psyche are not in principle bad, but they need the direction of reason so that they do not disrupt the overall harmony. According to Plato, we find peace of mind only when a harmony between passion and reason is attained. Given this framework, personal justice consists of harmony in the psyche, whereby each part of the psyche performs the function assigned to it by nature. Similarly, civic justice consists of harmony in society, whereby each person performs the duties for which he or she is by nature suited. The common good is not simply something that each member *receives*; the common good is something that each member *performs*. Plato envisioned a society in which each member according to his or her natural abilities and talents makes a contribution to society as a whole. He was concerned about a certain pattern of interaction among the citizens of society. In a just society where the common good is promoted, every citizen should enjoy a measure of prosperity and happiness and should contribute to the prosperity and happiness of others. Finally, the structural similarity between psychic life and civic life is rooted in a transcendent, eternal pattern. The harmony of the psyche and that of the city-state reflect the harmony of the transcendent realm of ideas. There is in Plato's mind a transcendent moral order to which the individual and society as a whole are to conform. It is at this point that Plato touches on the notion of *natural law*, which was later developed fully by the Stoics and which found expression in Cicero's *On the Laws* and *On the Commonwealth*. With regard to self-actualization, the main point that we can learn from Plato is this: The best that a particular person can be will always be the best in relation to the whole.

Already in the process of self-actualization, the relationships of the self to others are being transformed since self-actualization can only occur in a network of relationships. Nevertheless, the *process of the transformation of relationships* is distinguished from the process of self-actualization in that it aims specifically at attaining a balance between individualization and socialization. The absolutely individualized self, i.e. the self that at every point is true to itself, is an unsustainable ideal. The self may theoretically attain maximum individualization, but it ultimately destroys itself through the lack of social relationships. On the other hand, the absolutely socialized self is also unsustainable because it loses itself in the group and ceases to be an authentic individual. Therefore, both individualization and socialization of the self are necessary for the stability and health of the person. The individualization of the self takes place as the self discovers and asserts its uniqueness, whereas the socialization of the self occurs through active participation in groups such as families, friends, religious organizations and so forth.

Consider, for example, the development of a young child. As the child develops, the self goes through various phases in the process of maturation. During the early months of life, the child cannot distinguish clearly between itself and its mother, but as the child matures, the self becomes progressively more centered and more stable so that it is able to question its world and to seek its own peculiar identity in its surroundings. There is, however, a limit to the uniqueness that the self can develop in comparison with its world. As children, we don't choose the language that we will speak, it is literally our "mother" tongue. Similarly, the self adopts the manners and morals as well as the cognitive and behavioral patterns of its social environment. In this way, the self becomes integrated into a particular society. In the best possible case, the adult develops a self with a strong sense of individuality, but at the same time, a self that is well integrated into society. In the worst possible case, the self maximizes individualization, but destroys its relationships to others in the process, thus destroying itself. Or the self maximizes socialization and destroys itself by forfeiting its individuality. The natural law (lex naturalis), which we are explicating, requires that we find a healthy balance between individualization and socialization. Admittedly, such a balance is difficult to attain, and it is never attained once and for all. Throughout our entire lives, we are continually in the process of establishing this balance. Every one of us has had the experience of facing a situation in which we had to make a decision between "going along" with the group in order to promote our socialization and "defying" the group in order to preserve our individuality. Finding the right balance is a life-long process.

The process of the transformation of relationships concerns not only the individual person, but also society as a whole and its political structures. In Book VIII of the *Republic*, Plato discusses the transformation (or degeneration) of the Greek city-state from one form of government to another. In this context, he mentions five possible constitutional forms: the aristocratic, the timocratic, the oligarchic, the democratic and the tyrannical forms of government. The aristocratic form of government, whereby the educated upper class rule, is in Plato's mind the ideal, and the remaining four types are considered to be degenerate forms. The ruling power in the timocratic form is held by the honor-loving warriors, in the oligarchic form by the pleasure-loving few, in the democratic form by the liberty-loving masses and in the tyrannical form by an unscrupulous and ruthless individual. The aristocratic form of government is transformed into the timocratic form when the warrior class prevails over the intellectual class and imposes a militant policy dictated by ambition and the love of glory. The timocratic form is transformed into an oligarchy when those who love honor turn to money-grubbing. The oligarchic form is transformed into democracy when the poor in the oligarchic city-state revolt and insist on the liberty to do as they wish. Finally, the democratic form is transformed into tyranny when the liberty of democracy degenerates into lawlessness. To restore order, a strong leader is appointed who then raises an army to repress the lawless elements of society, thus establishing a tyrannical form of government.

As we know, Plato was not optimistic about the possibilities of a successful democracy, and he argued that the aristocratic form would be the ideal if a philosopher-king were in charge. The person who is both philosopher and king combines within himself wisdom and power and is thus able to make decisions that are just and good. No such form of government was ever instituted in Athens, and most interpreters consider Plato's suggestion to be totally unrealistic. Nevertheless, his extended dialogue on the various transformations of government has remained an important source for the study of political philosophy. The transformation from one form to another involves in each case fundamental changes in the relationships of individuals to society as well as in the structures of the society itself. Whereas the process of transformation on a personal level aims at attaining a balance between individualization and socialization, it moves on the societal level toward a balance between the well-being of the citizenry as a whole and the stability of governmental structures. The process of transformation of relationships on a societal level can occur very slowly over a long period of time or very quickly as in the case of a revolution.

The American Revolution of 1776 remains one of the prime examples in Western civilization of a successful transformation from one form of government to another. On the eve of the American Revolution, we find four distinct regional cultures in Colonial America: the Massachusetts Bay, the Chesapeake Bay, the Delaware Valley and the Appalachian highlands.[26] Each of these regions was populated by immigrants who came from different parts of Britain and who were culturally distinct long before their migration. There were dialectical differences in their speech, which were similar to the differences today between the Bostonian and the Southern dialectics, and there was also a religious diversity—these immigrants being either Puritans, Anglicans, Quakers or Evangelicals. All of this notwithstanding, they did have one thing in common: They were all immigrants seeking a better life in a new land. They were willing to leave their homeland with all of its familiarity and to travel great distances in the hope of finding something better.

Following the Revolutionary War, the four regional cultures found themselves in conflict with each other. To be sure, they had obtained their freedom from England, but they were still in the process of transformation from one form of government to another, i.e. from Colonial America to the United States of America. Eventually, the regions found a consensus through the careful formulation of the Constitution of 1787. As the Constitution clearly indicates, the United States was never intended to be a direct democracy; in spite of the talk today about spreading democracy in the world, the US was established from the beginning as a Republic, adopting certain ideas about human rights and property from the English philosopher John Locke. The phrase "Life, Liberty and the Pursuit of Happiness" in the Declaration of Independence served well to inspire the colonists to revolution, but when the Bill of Rights was added to the Constitution, the founders abandoned this phrase and took over the Lockean version emphasizing the right of "Life, Liberty and *Property*". The protection of property is typically a concern of those who *have* it, not of the poor who *don't have* it; for the "Have Nots", the right to pursue happiness would have been more important. From this, it is apparent that the US Republic had from its inception an aristocratic tendency, and yet, there have been Americans who truly wanted a democracy and have fought for a democracy. Martin Luther King, Jr. was one of them; Howard Zinn was another. So perhaps, it is not yet chiseled in stone that the United States will remain a republic instead of a democracy; constitutions can be amended or even altered through judicial interpretation. Like the process of transformation on the *personal* plane, the process of transformation of a *society* and of its government on a historical level is never complete.

The urgent need in the United States for a fundamental transformation on the political level can be seen from the following considerations. In the course of our discussion on self-actualization, it has become apparent that the self cannot actualize itself authentically without a consideration of the whole, i.e. without considering the social network in which the self lives. Likewise, a political system that does not consider the whole, i.e.

the well-being of the entire body of its citizens, is ultimately unsustainable. This is true of both a republic and a democracy. Unfortunately, the political system in the US has developed in such a way that neither democrats nor republicans focus any longer on the whole. The word "republic" comes from the Latin *res publica* and is often translated as "commonwealth". In true republicanism, there is a concern for the common-wealth, for the well-being of each and every citizen. True republicans should be defending the common good; otherwise, they are abandoning the *res publica* that they claim to be defending. On the other hand, the word "democracy" comes from the Greek *demokratia* meaning that the common people (*demos*) rule (*krateo*), which should mean by definition that democrats strive toward the common good. The major differences between the republicans and the democrats should be their political philosophy concerning the best way to secure the common good, but in actual fact, both parties have lost view of the whole and are focusing on particular interest groups. Whether it is the group of the wealthiest Americans, the group of the business leaders, the group of gays and lesbians, the group of Hispanics—whether it is this or that group is to some extent irrelevant; focusing on any group to the exclusion of the whole is not sustainable and will eventually result in a transformation to another form, perhaps to a much less desirable one.

If we pose the question concerning the underlying cause of the myopic perspective of both Republicans and Democrats, we find that the answer lies in the peculiar understanding of human rights and liberty that had held sway in the US since its founding. In contrast to Western Europe, the understanding of human rights in the US is characterized by an extreme individualism and absolutism. In the thinking of most Americans, the *individual* possesses certain *absolute* rights, and to the extent that groups come into view, the group is considered as a collection of individuals with absolute rights. The duties and responsibilities of the group in question are rarely mentioned, and the relationship between human rights and the common good is, in most cases, not a topic of discussion. In the following chapter, we will consider this problem in greater detail.

Chapter 6

Natural Right, Human Rights and the Common Good

In *Citizens of the Broken Compass* (2015), I proposed the thesis that societies are partially and sometimes even predominately defined by the way in which they understand the relationship between *individual interests* and the *common good*. Both of these concepts require definition. How does the society in question define the common good? As the collective well-being of its citizens? Or perhaps as the strength of its government? And how does the society define the individual interests of its citizens? As individual human rights? Or as the quality of life of each citizen? Obviously, there are quite a few possibilities for both of these concepts. Considering the situation of the United States today, one might venture the assertion that the common good has been defined as *national security*, whereas the supreme individual interest has been defined as the inalienable human right that we call *freedom*. Once a society has defined these terms, the relationship between them becomes a matter of considerable concern; in some cases the relationship may seem almost self-evident, but in other cases it may prove to be quite problematic. In the case of national security and freedom, the relationship has resulted in heated debate about the possibility of balancing the two. It is far from obvious how the government can guarantee security to its citizens and, at the same time, protect the individual freedoms of its citizens.

In societies of antiquity like the Athenian Democracy and the Roman Republic as well as in many later pre-modern societies, the problem of balancing individual interests and the common good was much less acute than it is today. The reason for this lies in the fact that the pre-modern theory of natural right (*ius naturale*) united the two in a more or less harmonious fashion. What was in the interest of the individual citizen was considered to be also in the interest of the citizenry as a whole. If this idea sounds strange to our ears, it is because we are living on the other side of the chasm that separates modern from classical thought. Historically, we can see how this chasm began to open in the seventeenth century with the erosion of the harmony between individual interests and the common good. Under the pressure of scientific thought in the seventeenth century and then the Enlightenment in the eighteenth century, the theory of natural right broke apart so that natural right (*ius naturale*) became human rights (*iures humana*) and the common good became concentrated in the absolute power of the monarchy. The period of European history between the end of the Thirty Years' War (1648) and beginning of the French Revolution (1789) is commonly termed the "Age of Absolutism" because political power and legal authority in many countries were concentrated in the hands of monarchs. Monarchs claimed for themselves the authority to issue laws, to collect taxes, to declare war and peace and so forth. Furthermore, they propagated the idea that their absolute power was synonymous with the common good of society. That is, the old notion of the common good was used to justify the absolute power of the monarch.

It is in this context that the political philosophy of Thomas Hobbes (1588–1679) is to be interpreted. In his famous book *Leviathan* (1651), Hobbes justifies the absolute power of the monarch by arguing that the exercise of individual rights in the original state of nature led ultimately to a condition of perpetual war. Since such a state of war was unsustainable, individuals renounced their rights contractually and established monarchies of absolute power. The political philosophy of Hobbes was in many ways determinative for European thought, and its influence extended well into the eighteenth century. But the eighteenth century was not monolithic; it also witnessed a countermovement to the absolutism of monarchs. In the Enlightenment, writers such as Jean-Jacques Rousseau (1712–1778) extolled the rational ability of human beings and promoted the idea of individual rights of human beings as a protection against the absolutist claims of monarchs. In the United States, one thinks immediately of the Declaration of Independence (1776), which claimed for the colonists the inalienable rights of life, liberty and the pursuit of happiness against the authority of King George III of England. Following on the heels of the American Revolution was the French Revolution of 1789 with its cry of "Liberty, Equality, Fraternity" against the absolutism of King Louis XVI. As a matter of historical record, it is interesting to note that the original concept of human rights developed as a reaction to the claims of the State; individual human rights were intended to protect the individual against the abuses of an absolute monarchy. With this brief overview of the dissolution of the concept of natural right, we turn now to a more detailed discussion of our topic.

In Chapter 2, we investigated the concept of *law* in classical Greek thought and traced its development from pre-Socratic philosophers like Heraclitus down to the Stoic ideas found in the writings of Cicero. In his book *On the Laws*, Cicero gives the most complete account of the Stoic concept of natural law (*lex naturalis*) that is still extant. When we use the word "law", we usually mean the written laws of the state that are formulated and promulgated by legislators. However, before any state was constituted or any law was written, there was, according to Cicero, the highest law in nature, which he identified with reason. Reason in nature and reason in the human mind are the same, and Cicero refers to both as the highest law. Since this law permeates all things, it binds all people together into a common world city.

Significantly, Cicero employs the terms "natural law" (*lex naturalis*) and "natural right" (*ius naturale*) in many contexts synonymously, although natural right had in general a broader meaning for him than natural law. Linguistically, the word *ius* meaning "right" was the root from which "just" (*iustus*) and "justice" (*iustitia*) were derived.[27(pxl)] So "natural right" (*ius naturale*) always had the connotation of justice or fairness. On the other hand, "natural law" (*lex naturalis*) referred to right reason, which was thought to permeate the universe and to dictate to the human mind that which is commanded to be done and that which is prohibited. In order to simplify the matter, we could say that natural law is always grounded in natural right and is therefore always fair and just.

If we look for the historical roots of the modern idea of *human rights*, we discover that the notion can be traced back to Stoic concept of *natural right*. Nevertheless, the differences between the Stoic idea of "right" and our idea of "rights" are striking. According to the Stoics, the entire cosmos is permeated by an eternal moral law or natural right that guaranties justice. The Stoics spoke about the natural right (*ius naturale*) that guided the actions of human beings, and those individuals who lived in accordance with natural right were said to be virtuous, that is, morally good. In *On the Laws* Cicero has an extended section on natural law or natural right in which he maintains that right reason or natural right in the universe binds all human beings together and obligates them to strive after justice. We as human beings are born with a sense of natural right and wrong, and therefore to be truly human, we must exercise justice in relating to each other. The connectivity of all human beings through natural right means that individual interests and the common good cannot ultimately be separated. In his book *On Duties*, Cicero writes:

If (a person) thinks that acting violently against other men involves doing nothing contrary to nature—then how can you argue with him? For he takes all of the "human" out of a human...Therefore all men should have this one object, that the *benefit of each individual* and the *benefit of all together* should be the same.[9(3.26f)] (Italics added)

We are prone by nature to love our fellow human beings[7(1.34f)], and anyone who denies justice to another person destroys something within himself[8(3.33)]. So the idea of natural right unified the interests of the individual and the common good.

In summary, the Stoic idea of natural right was *cosmic*, rather than *individual*. To be sure, natural right motivated a person to action—not, however, in the sense of insisting on one's own rights, but rather in the sense of obligating one to act in a certain way. Natural right was not a *claimed* right, but rather an *obligating* right. It was not a purely subjective possession of the individual, but rather an objective order of the universe governing the individual's conduct. Finally, the individual's conduct in accordance with natural right was thought to promote the benefit of all citizens. In his *On the Commonwealth*, Cicero writes: "Well then: the commonwealth (*res publica*) is the concern (*res*) of a people, but a people is not just any group of men assembled in any way, but an assemblage of some size associated with one another through agreement on law (*ius*) and a partnership for the common benefit".[8(1.39)]

The modern development of Cicero's concepts of natural law and natural right is striking. As we saw in Chapter 2, the concept of natural law (*lex naturalis*) ceased in the seventeenth century to have any moral or ethical meaning and was adopted by scientists in order to explain the physical regularities of nature. Thus natural law (*lex naturalis*) was transformed into the laws of nature (*leges naturae*). After the moral law of nature became the scientific laws of nature, natural right (*ius naturale*) became human rights (*iures humana*), as we know them today. The parallel development is interesting because it reveals the common root of our scientific and political thought. Both the laws of nature, which are a part of our scientific view of the world, and human rights, which are the only universally accepted moral standard in Western societies, can be traced back to the Stoic notion of reason permeating the universe.

The transition from an understanding of natural right as an objective, governing principle to an understanding of human rights as a subjective claim on others took place over several centuries, but the most significant changes occurred in the seventeenth century. In the writings of Thomas Hobbes, the modern concept of human rights begins to emerge clearly: a natural right understood as a *claim*, not as a *duty*. Equally clear is that this transition took place under the influence of the emerging classical physics of the seventeenth century. What was groundbreaking in the political philosophy of Thomas Hobbes was his application of Galileo's investigation of the motion of bodies and the latter's atomistic view of matter to an understanding of the commonwealth. Hobbes assumed that in the original state of nature human beings were like atoms; each one had certain innate rights, but they were not bound together into a community. That is to say, the *individual*, not the *community*, was for Hobbes the fundamental fact of nature, and the right of nature was something that the individual possessed, not something that governed the conduct of society. In his *Leviathan* (1651), Hobbes writes:

> The RIGHT OF NATURE, which Writers commonly call *Jus Naturale*, is the Liberty each man hath, to use his own power, as he will himselfe, for the preservation of his own Nature; that is to say, of his own Life; and consequently, of doing any thing, which in his own Judgment, and Reason, hee shall conceive to be the aptest means thereunto.[28(p91)]

According to Hobbes, the state of nature is one in which every individual has a right to everything he deems necessary for survival. Since there are no restrictions on this fundamental right of nature, the state of nature turns out to be one of constant war. Everyone has a right to everything, and the conflicting rights lead necessarily to perpetual war. In order to attain a peaceful coexistence, all individuals must agree contractually to give up their natural right to everything. Hobbes' right of nature is clearly a *claim-right*, not a *duty-right*. My right to preserve my own life gives me the right to claim whatever means are necessary to that end. In this context, the obligation of natural right in Cicero's sense loses its meaning.

As we have stated, Hobbes relied to a large extent on the physics of Galileo in developing his political thought; specifically, he found in the notion of individual atoms a model for understanding society. Galileo died in 1642, and about a year later, Sir Isaac Newton was born. In many ways, Newton brought the work of scientists like Kepler and Galileo to a conclusion in that he developed a comprehensive understanding of the motion of bodies. More important for the present discussion, however, is the fact that Newton followed Galileo in rejecting the medieval, Aristotelian conception of the world and in adopting the Epicurean understanding that the world is composed of atoms. In the second edition of his *Opticks*, Newton writes:

All these things being considered, it seems probable to me, that God in the beginning formed matter in solid, massy, hard, impenetrable, moveable particles; of such sizes and figures, and with such other properties, and in such proportion to space, as most conduced to the end for which he formed them; and that these primitive particles being solids, are incomparably harder than any Porous bodies compounded of them; even so very hard, as never to wear or break in pieces: no ordinary power being able to divide what God himself made One, in the first creation.[14(p260)]

In developing an atomistic, mechanistic view of the world, Newton lent indirect support to the political philosophy of Hobbes. Just as the basic building block of the physical world is the atom, the fundamental building block of society is the individual with his right of nature to self-preservation.

The political philosophy of Thomas Hobbes has had a tremendous impact on Western societies. The understanding of the individual as the building block of society and the concomitant emphasis on individual rights are the roots of many contemporary moral and political points of view. However, Hobbes was not the only political philosopher who contributed to the modern concept of human rights. Particularly in Continental Europe, Jean-Jacques Rousseau was a major influence in the eighteenth century, and the differences between the US and the European understanding of human rights are to a great extent the result of the divergent views of these two philosophers. In her excellent book *Rights Talk: The Impoverishment of Political Discourse* (1991), Mary Ann Glendon discusses in detail the peculiar characteristics of the US concept of rights that negatively distinguish it from the concept in Western Europe. She writes: "The exaggerated absoluteness of our American rights rhetoric is closely bound up with its other distinctive traits—a near-silence concerning responsibility, and a tendency to envision the rights-bearer as a lone autonomous individual."[29(p45)] Even the rights of the family tend to be understood in terms of the rights of its individual members rather than as the rights of the family as a unit. To the extent that groups of individuals are considered in the context of human rights, it is always a matter of particular "interest groups", i.e. "collections of self-seeking individuals pursuing limited, parallel, aims".[29(p115)] In such cases, the understanding of the rights-bearer remains the same; the individual is "radically alone" and "naturally at odds with his fellows".[29(p115)] Clearly, these formulations echo the philosophy of Thomas Hobbes and help to explain why interest groups have difficulty working for the common good. For example, the gay/lesbian movement never really focuses on the common good of society, but rather on the individual rights of its members; likewise, major corporations do not focus on the common good of society, but rather on the proprietary rights of their stockholders.

In contrast, the European political philosophy preserved more of the pre-modern emphasis on the societal dimension of human existence. To be sure, modern Europeans focus much more on the individual than they did before the Enlightenment, but the classical tradition (Plato, Aristotle, Cicero etc.) left an indelible mark on the European mentality that is still reflected in an understanding of the individual embedded in society. In discussing West European constitutions and charters framed after the Second World War, Glendon writes:

> In the implicit anthropology, so to speak, of these charters, each human being's freedom and individuality is recognized as entitled to the highest respect. But men and women are also seen as essentially social beings, situated within relationships. People do not "enter" society; they are constituted in part by society and in turn constitute it.[29(p74)]

The individual is not viewed as a loner who is self-sufficient and self-determining, but rather as a member of society who is dependent on others and in turn responsible to others.

The uniqueness of the American understanding of human rights is well illustrated by a comparison of the US Bill of Rights with the United Nations Universal Declaration of Human Rights. According to the latter, "Everyone has duties to the community" and the rights of individuals are subject to limitations "for the purpose of securing due recognition and respect for the rights and freedoms of others and of meeting the just requirements of morality, public order and the general welfare in a democratic society" (Article 29). In the Bill of Rights of the United States, we find numerous claim-rights, including free speech and the bearing of arms, and in Amendment V the well-known phrase: nor shall any person "be deprived of life, liberty, or property, without due process of law". But nowhere in the Bill of Rights do we find an indication of the duties and responsibilities of citizenship. This absence of language expressing duties and responsibilities together with the lack of concern for the common good in society has imbued the notion of rights in the US with an absoluteness that is not only problematic, but in some cases totally untenable. That the emphasis on the isolated individual and his absolute rights can lead to unresolvable conflict is clear in the case of the debate over abortion. Here we have a conflict of right against right, the right of the expectant mother and the right of the fetus. On an international level, we have an apparently unresolvable conflict between two groups of people in the Middle East, one claiming the right of self-defense and security, the other claiming the right of self-determination and freedom. Within the context of human rights, both claims seem to be legit- imate, and yet the claims taken together lead us into an impasse. In order to resolve such conflicts, we need an additional perspective that supplements the one-sided notion of human rights.

Not only is the concept of human rights problematic in actual practice, but the advancement of theoretical physics in the twentieth century has made it abundantly clear that the atomistic, mechanistic view of the world that underpinned individual rights is untenable. Atoms are not the ultimate building blocks of the physical world, and the self-sufficient individual is not the ultimate building block of society; there is connectivity in the universe that mandates a return to a more holistic view of society, specifically to the notion of the *common good*.

A discussion of the specific scientific developments that

altered the context of our thinking lies beyond the scope of the present work, but for those readers who are interested in physics, it should be apparent that I am alluding to the phenomenon of quantum entanglement and non-locality. In order to approach the phenomenon intuitively, let us imagine a time before modern communication when messages from Europe to the United States took a considerable amount of time. We imagine further that there is a married couple living in New York City and another married couple living in Zurich, Switzerland. The New York couple enjoys every morning at eight o'clock either a cup of coffee or a cup of tea, but neither both on the same day. The Zurich couple enjoys every afternoon at two o'clock either a cup of coffee or a cup of tea, but neither both on the same day. Now we keep a log of the events on both sides of the Atlantic—whether the New York couple has coffee or tea and whether the Zurich couple has coffee or tea—and what we discover is astonishing. Without exception, when the New York couple has coffee, the Zurich couple has tea. And when the New York couple has tea, the Zurich couple has coffee. Since there is a six hour time difference between New York and Zurich, the correlated events are taking place at the same time, and therefore, there is no possibility of communication between the two. A causal connection is excluded, but nevertheless, the events are perfectly correlated. This analogy gives us an intuitive understanding of what is happening on the quantum level of reality.

At the quantum level, the idea of location in space no longer has any meaning because nothing is ultimately separable from anything else. Physicists have termed this situation non-locality or non-separability of quantum reality. Considering that everything in our immediate physical environment is made up of quanta that have been interacting with other quanta since the Big-Bang, the quantum reality of non-separability must be understood as fundamental to *our* reality. Whether one wants to speak of a deeper reality or a transcendent reality, the fact is inescapable: There is a reality more fundamental than the one we perceive with the five senses—a reality that is not restricted by time and space and in which non-causal interactions occur because everything is ultimately connected.

Such revolutionary discoveries in quantum physics have placed Newtonian physics in a new light. Was the classical physics of Newton wrong? The answer to this question is: yes and no. On the level of everyday experience, the basic principles that we learn in an introductory physics course are totally adequate. If we are calculating the velocity of a falling object or if we are building a bridge, the laws of classical physics are applicable. If, however, we are dealing with a situation on the subatomic level, the classical laws are no longer accurate. Likewise, if we ask the question whether the concept of human rights is wrong, the answer must be: yes and no. In many situations, the notion of human rights is very useful and can lead to morally responsible results, but human rights must always be seen against the background of the common good. As we have seen, the traditional concept of natural right united individual interests and the common good, and if this union is no longer a possibility in our world, we need at least a counterbalance to the notion of human rights. That is, we need some sense of the common good in order to lead us out of the impasse of conflicting rights.

By emphasizing natural law and the common good, we are not advocating a return to Stoic philosophy or to the political thought of Cicero. The pre-scientific idea of a timeless moral law or an unchanging common good in the universe is in the twenty-first century no longer tenable. Rather, we are maintaining that some sense of the common good is necessary as a complement to the concept of human rights. Clearly, neither natural law nor the common good need be timeless and unchanging, although they must be relatively stable in a particular culture and in a particular historical period. Furthermore, a new orientation toward the common good must take into account an understanding of nature in general as well as human nature in particular. Only in this way can the notion of the common good be protected from interpretations that ultimately ignore the welfare of the citizenry as a whole. In this regard, one thinks immediately of the fascist philosophy of the Second World War that set the good of the nation above the good of the people comprising the nation. Another such abuse is the "trickle-down" theory of economics that claims benefits for all citizens if the upper income earners prosper. Both of these concepts of the common good fail on the grounds that they lack real connectivity. A fascist governmental structure does not translate into benefits for all—a fact that was very apparent in Germany during the years of National Socialism. And the theory of "trickle-down" economics has conspicuously resulted in a concentration of wealth in the upper one percent of the population, leaving many workers anxious and unsure about their future. If we heed the natural world—not just the biological realm of Darwinism, but nature in its most fundamental state—, then we discover that connectivity is essential for the common good. If one prefers, we can term connectivity in the human realm "relatedness". The fundamental relatedness of individuals is essential for human existence and thus for the common good of human beings.

If we expand our understanding of the common good to include not only physical nature, but also human nature, we find that the relatedness essential for the common good must be combined with our basic insights into the structure of the self. Just as the balancing of the polarities force-power, time-eternity and life-spirit establishes a stable self and promotes *excellence of life*, the processes of self-knowledge, self-actualization and trans-formation of relationships promote the *common good*. If we were to broaden our definition of individual interests so that the primary interest of the individual consisted in obtaining excel-lence of life, then there would be no real tension between individual interests and the common good. Otherwise stated, the attainment of individual interests would necessarily advance the common good. The balancing of the polarities of the self would be expressed in society as the successful processes of self-knowledge, self-actualization and restoration of relationships. Such an interpretation would move us very close to the traditional view of human nature and society, but at this point in our history, it will be necessary to retain the current understanding of individual interests as formulated in the concept of human rights and to view the common good as a corrective to the absoluteness of human rights.

Chapter 7

Natural Law and Moral Guideposts

In the previous chapters, we have attempted to outline a new understanding of natural law using as our starting point the concept of the self. We defined the self as the center of experience in the individual, and this center of experience is characterized first and foremost by identity—what we call self-identity. Furthermore, the self-identity of the individual consists of two elements: unity and continuity. I experience myself as one self (unity), not as two or three, and I experience myself as the same self today as I was yesterday or last year (continuity). Unlike our physical bodies and the structure of our brains, our self-identity is not simply a given in our lives. We must establish it. Much of the identity building of the self is unconscious, and there are many cultural and environmental factors that continually come into play. Still, if we search beneath the details, we find that there are three polarities which are operative in the formation of self-identity: force-power, time-eternity, and life-spirit. Depending on the way in which these polarities are weighted, the identity of the self will acquire this or that form. For instance, the polarities can be unbalanced to the point that the individual experiences consciously only one side of them; the individual experiences force, time and life very clearly, but power, eternity and spirit only very vaguely. In the ideal case, however, the polarities are brought into a healthy balance. Since as human beings we are bound to balance these polarities in some way in order to establish our self-identity, they constitute the most fundamental layer of natural law.

There is, however, another dimension to natural law. The self of the individual is never abstracted from the world in which it is embedded; the self is always a self in *relation* to a world. For this reason, natural law has not only a personal, but also a societal dimension. In relating to society, the polarities of natural law become processes: self-knowledge, self-actualization and the transformation of relationships. Self-knowledge cannot be attained if the self is cut off from all relationships. The picture of an individual living totally alone from birth onward and attaining thereby a profound understanding of him- or herself is completely unrealistic. Without a network of relationships, the isolated individual would not even acquire language, and without language, self-knowledge is impossible. The attainment of self-knowledge requires the presence of the Other in the immediate world of the self. With the attainment of self-knowledge of one's own innate capabilities and intrinsic limitations, the process of self-actualization has already begun. Nevertheless, self-actualization takes place primarily in a network of relationships in society that extend far beyond the Other of self-knowledge. Just as the natural law obligates us to strive toward self-knowledge, it also places upon us the obligation to develop the innate potentialities that we possess. We are to become the very best human beings that we are capable of becoming. But the very best that we can become is always the best that we can become in relation to the whole of society. For this reason, the actualization of innate potentialities must always have the common good in view. As we actualize ourselves, the relationships of the self to others are being transformed since self-actualization can only occur in a network of relationships. Nonetheless, the process of the transformation of relationships is distinguished from the process of self-actualization in that it aims specifically at attaining a balance between individualization and socialization. The absolutely individualized self, i.e. the self that at every point is true to itself, is an unsustainable ideal. The self attains maximum individualization, but ultimately destroys itself through the lack of social relationships. On the other hand, the absolutely socialized self is also unsustainable because it loses itself in the group and ceases to be an authentic individual. Therefore, both individualization and socialization of the self are necessary for the stability and health of the person. The individualization of the self is accomplished through the establishment of a strong self-identity with distinct contours, whereas the socialization of the self takes place through participation in groups such as families, friends and religious organizations. When the transformation of relationships reaches the highest level where entire societies and governments are transformed, the process aims at the establishment of structures and policies for the benefit of all citizens. At this point, it becomes abundantly clear that the ultimate goal of natural law is the attainment of the common good.

In summary, natural law (*lex naturalis*) requires that we *balance* the polarities of the self (force-power, time-eternity and life-spirit) and that we *strive* for the common good through the processes of self-knowledge, self-actualization and the transformation of relationships. In Western societies, however, characterized as they are by stress and distraction, it seems unlikely that the knowledge alone of natural law will lead to any significant progress. Therefore, we are proposing certain *guideposts* for compliance with natural law. As the word "guidepost" suggests, we are not formulating rules, but rather providing indicators for fulfilling natural law. These *guideposts* for compliance with natural law are: *respectful dialogue, opportuneness of action* and *community-building*. It should be apparent that these guideposts are related to natural law in the following way: respectful dialogue corresponds to the polarity force-power and to the process of self-knowledge; opportuneness of action to the polarity time-eternity and to the process of self-actualization; and finally community-building to the polarity life-spirit and the process of transformation of relationships.

Let us consider now in more detail the moral guideposts with some reference to particular issues. Perhaps the most distinguishing factor about *respectful dialogue* is that it requires the active engagement of two or more persons. Just as the Other is essential for the attainment of self-knowledge, other persons are essential for any type of dialogue. Monologues are not dialogues. Unfortunately, monologues have become a dominant mode of communication in the age of technology. Bumper stickers may communicate a message, but they do not offer the possibility of dialogue. Regardless of one's position on politics and religion, messages on the bumper of an automobile that read "Keep Christ in Christmas", "Support our Troops" and so forth do not promote respectful dialogue. These bumper stickers simply shout a message at total strangers, without allowing a response; they lack dignity and are certainly not respectful of others. Many political advertisements fall into the same category. They stem from a bumper sticker mentality that is either unable or unwilling to participate in respectful dialogue. Authentic dialogue requires that individuals invest the time and energy to converse with each other, sometimes on difficult issues where opinions may differ considerably. Dialogue is demanding and can even be exhausting, but respectful dialogue is a necessary guidepost to moral conduct.

Yet, *respectful* dialogue requires more than just a willingness to listen to others. Every one of us has been in a situation where a supposed "dialogue" turned out to be nothing more than two monologues. Each participant spoke his or her mind and then listened patiently until the next opportunity presented itself to regain control of the dialogue. Such a "dialogue" may appear to be an advance over the bumper sticker communication, but in reality, it is not significantly different. If Mr Jones says that he agrees with the viewpoint of a particular political commentator on a current issue and Mrs Smith says that she does not agree, this is not yet a dialogue between two individuals. Respectful dialogue requires not only that we listen patiently while the other speaks; it requires that we actually consider the other person's viewpoint and empathize with it to the extent that we can. We must temporarily set aside our own point of view and consider the matter from the point of view of the other person. We must weigh carefully his or her opinion on the matter, search out the best elements in it and find, if possible, some common ground for discussion. In the end, we may return to our original point of view and to the opinions with which we began, but in most cases, the dialogue will have resulted in some modification. Too often, conversations between persons of opposed positions are understood to be contests in order to determine who is right. In respectful dialogue, however, there is no winner because it is not a contest; for all parties involved, it is a process of clarification which is necessary in order to make morally responsible decisions. In an age of sound bites and bumper stickers, such dialogue is indeed a rarity, but unless we are able to cultivate it in the future, we are doomed to react like the "herd" described by the group psychologists—the herd that is easily led this or that way by the latest propaganda.

Our second guidepost is the *opportuneness of action*. Of the three guideposts, this one is the most conspicuously temporal in nature. What is opportune is that which fits the present circumstances. "It was an opportune moment", we say. An *opportune* offer of assistance is an offer occurring at an appropriate time. Should the offer be made at some other time, it may be unwelcome or even harmful, given the constellation of factors at that moment. An event must be timely or else it does not contribute to the common good. Thus, opportuneness is an element that should always be considered when we appeal to human rights. Human rights tend to be understood as relatively permanent. If individuals have human right "A" today, they have it tomorrow and next year as well. The question of the common good is this: is it opportune to claim this human right at this time? Or: is it opportune to grant this human right to this individual or to this group at this time? Naturally, individuals will often disagree about the opportuneness of claiming this or that right, but it is essential that the question be raised and openly discussed.

The Greeks of classical antiquity had a keen sense of temporal and spatial balance, which was reflected in their art, architecture, literature and philosophy. One of the enduring representations of their spatial sense of balance is the famous Parthenon atop the Acropolis in Athens. The temporal balance of Greek thinking found expression in the political and ethical dimension of their society. The usual word for "time" in classical Greek was *chronos*, from which we have the English word "chronology", but the Greek language contained a second word for "time" that has no direct counterpart in English. The *kairos* referred to the "decisive moment" in time for a person to take action; the *kairos* demands action and determines the life of the individual by challenging him at a critical moment in time. Particularly in the Stoic ethics of Epictetus (55–135 AD), the *kairos* became a moral demand on the individual, but even Cicero pointed to the *kairos* when he discussed the "opportuneness of occasions" in *On Duties*. He writes:

> Now I must say something about the orderliness of things, and the opportuneness of occasions... The opportune time for acting is called in Greek *eukairia*, and in Latin *occasio*. Consequently this type of moderateness, which we interpret as I have explained, is the knowledge of opportuneness, that is, of the fitting occasions for doing something.[9](1.142)

Inherent in the notion of the *kairos* is the element of waiting. The very fact that the *kairos* ("decisive moment") is distinct from the *chronos* ("time") implies a limitation on the opportuneness of action. The appropriate time of action is a window of opportunity that can suddenly appear and just as quickly vanish. Time (*chronos*) moves continually like a never-ending stream, but the critical moment of action (*kairos*) is not always present. One must watch and wait for the "right time". Such waiting is, however, not a passive experience; it is much more akin to the attentiveness of the well-trained waiter in a fine restaurant. A trained waiter does not interrupt the flow of the dinner, but is always present to act at the right moment. Similarly, one should not act before the *kairos*; an inopportune political action can be more disruptive than helpful to a society.

At this point, we must clarify an important issue in order to avoid any misunderstanding. Determining the opportuneness of action is not to be understood as a matter of divination, but rather as an endeavor of serious thought and critical reflection. By emphasizing the crucial role of the *kairos*, we are not moving into the area of religion, but rather into the area of historical investigation and interpretation. Only through the investigation and interpretation of history can we recognize what is appropriate at a particular point in time. Whether it is appropriate and opportune to recognize a particular right at a particular time cannot be determined by focusing myopically on a small segment of time and on a small group of individuals. As human beings we are a part of history, and the waters of history run very deep. We deceive ourselves when we think that we can control the *kairos*.

It was George Santayana, a former Professor of Philosophy at Harvard, who said: "Those who cannot learn from history are doomed to repeat it." But history is not simply a timeline of events, a chronical of what and where something happened. History is interrelatedness. History is a woven fabric of connections and meanings. In the United States, the 4th of July is usually celebrated as though it commemorated the founding of the country instead of the declaration of independence from England. The two events were, however, separate in time and significance. The Declaration of Independence of 1776 speaks of "life, liberty and the pursuit of happiness"; the US Constitution of 1787 speaks of "life, liberty and property". A chronical simply records these facts, but history raises questions about the connections and the meanings. Why was there a shift from "pursuit of happiness" to "protection of property"? Did Shays' Rebellion in Massachusetts play a role? And who were these men who called themselves "We, the people" in the Constitution? History is a fabric of connections and meanings and must be understood if we are to make responsible political and moral decisions. Any issue that is decided solely on the basis of human rights is framed too narrowly and cannot be adequately discussed. "Rights talk" tends to be punctilinear, i.e. it focuses on particular points in time and rarely broadens to an historical perspective. If we approach the issue from the standpoint of connections and meanings, we must raise different types of questions. Assuming that we acknowledge a particular right, what will be culturally lost or gained? What will be enabled or hindered? How will it affect our history? What are our expectations for the future? How far do the connections reach and what do they mean? Is it appropriate to grant this right at this time?

Consider, for instance, the flag-burning incident of 1984. The desecration of the American flag during a political demonstration was widely publicized as a legal case, but it also had a moral dimension that is relevant to the present discussion. At that time, there were prohibitions in 48 States against desecrating the American flag. At a political demonstration during the 1984 Republican National Convention in Dallas, Texas, Gregory Lee Johnson poured kerosene onto an American flag and set it on fire. He was arrested by the Dallas police and charged with desecrating the flag. The *Texas v. Johnson* case eventually went to the US Supreme Court in 1989, which ruled that Johnson had the right under the First Amendment to express his political views in this way. William Rehnquist wrote in his dissent:

The American flag, then, throughout more than 200 years of our history, has come to be the visible symbol embodying our

Nation. It does not represent the views of any particular political party, and does not represent any particular political party... Millions and millions of Americans regard it with an almost mystical reverence regardless of what sort of social, political, or philosophical beliefs they may have.

The intuition of Rehnquist may have been correct, but in the end, there was no way to defend the national symbol against "rights talk". The rights of an individual or a group almost always win, regardless of the long-term damage to society. Today, the American flag has ceased to be a symbol. It may be the logo of the United States, just as the golden arches are the logo of McDonald's. Waving the American flag seems to function as a means of identification, but the flag itself is no longer a powerful symbol. Otherwise, bikini swimwear with the stars and stripes would never be accepted by society. As far as the *Texas v. Johnson* case is concerned, it may well be that the US Supreme Court made the right decision from a purely legal standpoint. But from a moral standpoint, Gregory Lee Johnson himself and those who assisted him should have raised the question about the appropriateness of their action. Given the history of the United States and the significance of the flag, they were obligated to consider the question: Is this act of desecration really opportune? Regrettably, they did not, and to my knowledge, the media at the time was equally remiss. So in retrospect, we pose the question: Was it truly a response to the *kairos* of the time? Or was it a short-sighted expression of free speech that has had far-reaching and unforeseen consequences?

Similar questions could have been raised about the right of same-sex marriage, and in my opinion, they should have been raised and discussed thoroughly before the US Supreme Court ruled on the case. Whether the court's decision in *Obergefell v. Hodges*, whereby same-sex marriage was ruled to be a constitutional right, will be in the long term to the benefit or to the detriment of the US is a question that nobody can answer. For over 2500 years, Western civilizations have considered heterosexual marriage to be the norm, and this tradition was not simply the result of Christian influence. In both the Athenian Democracy and the Roman Republic, same-sex marriages were not accepted. Perhaps in our technological wisdom, we understand human nature and the world around us better that Plato, Aristotle, Cicero, Augustine, Thomas Aquinas and many others did. Perhaps they were wrong, and we are right. Unfortunately, the matter has been decided solely on the basis of human rights with little regard for the appropriateness of granting this right at this particular time in history. To be sure, attitudes in American society about same-sex marriage have shifted dramatically between the time of the "Stonewall Riots" in Greenwich Village and the US Supreme Court decision, but this shift had little to do with an investigation and interpretation of history or with a discernment of the *kairos*. The most obvious influence on public opinion was the film industry. Certainly by 1996 it was apparent that Hollywood had made the decision to support the gay/lesbian movement; in the outstanding movie *The Birdcage*, Robin Williams was able to move middle class attitudes beyond the disturbing events of the "Stonewall Riots" of 1969. Since then, the movie industry has encouraged the American public step by step to be more accepting of same-sex relationships and has brought the nation to the point of accepting, at least ostensibly, the Supreme Court decision. Without doubt, artistic expression has an important role to play in shaping public opinion, but it cannot and should not replace serious discussion among the citizens of a nation. Although artistic expression in the form of films has a tremendous impact on emotions, it fails to make critical rational distinctions that are necessary in order to make responsible decisions about issues affecting the future. Same-sex marriage is a very complex issue and should have been discussed on various levels: the *legal*, the *moral* and the *religious*. With regard to the moral dimension, the rights-bearers themselves, i.e. the gays and the lesbians, could have asked the question concerning the appropriateness of same-sex marriage at this point in time. When controversial questions are discussed openly and honestly, there is in general much less danger of a subsequent backlash. There is also less chance of negative reactions such as that of Kim Davis, the clerk in Rowan County, Kentucky. Soon after the US Supreme Court decision on same-sex marriage, she refused to issue a marriage license to a same-sex couple and was arrested on charges of contempt of court. She defended her actions by claiming that she is acting on "God's authority". Perhaps, such situations could have been avoided if we had discussed the differences between the legal, the moral and the religious before the Supreme Court ruling.

The last guidepost for the common good is *community-building*. In considering the rights of individuals or groups of individuals, it is important to evaluate the effect of such rights on the community as a whole. Will the granting of certain rights to a particular group build the community or divide it? Will the long-term effects be divisive or unifying? Since a society divided against itself cannot survive, it is imperative to reflect on the community as a whole in making decisions about rights. At first glance, the evaluation of community-building would seem to be rather straightforward. That which divides the community is destructive and that which unites the community is constructive. Yet, a closer look at the matter leads to considerations that are far from obvious. If we consider "dividing" or "uniting" in terms of public opinion, we begin to realize that public opinion can easily be manipulated through modern techniques of propaganda, giving the appearance of a united community, where in fact no community really exists. The word "community" is derived from classical Latin (*communitas*) and carries the meaning of a fellowship or society of individuals who share certain things in common. The community shares a common history as well as common social, economic and political interests. It shares certain opinions and attitudes, but just as important as the ideas that are held in common is the *sharing* itself, i.e. the communication of ideas among members of the society. *Communication and community go hand in hand.* With the rise of mass psychology around the turn of the twentieth century and the ensuring development of advertising and public relations, the normal functioning of communication within communities has been fundamentally altered so that authentic community-building has been replaced to a great extent by consensus-building through the manipulation of public opinion.

The modern history of public relations began after the end of the First World War with the work of Edward Bernays, the nephew of Sigmund Freud. Although Bernays was born in 1891 in Vienna, Austria, his family immigrated to the United States in 1892 where English became his mother tongue. Over the years, Bernays maintained contact with his uncle Sigmund and incorporated fundamental ideas of depth psychology into his methods of propaganda. During the First World War, Bernays had worked in the "Committee on Public Information" under the direction of George Creel—a committee that was charged by President Woodrow Wilson with the task of supporting the war effort. After the War, Bernays wrote in his book *Propaganda* (1928):

It was, of course, the astounding success of propaganda during the war that opened the eyes of the *intelligent few* in all departments of life to the possibilities of regimenting the public mind... It was only natural, after the war ended, that intelligent persons should ask themselves whether it was possible to apply a similar technique to the problems of peace... This new technique may fairly be called the new propaganda.[30(p54)] (Italics added)

In this passage, it is clear that the methods of Bernays were intended to aid the elite of society ("intelligent few") in manipulating the general public in order to manufacture consent.

Concomitant with Bernays' interests in assisting the elite was his disdain for the general public. Following the mass psychology of Gustave Le Bon (*Psychologie des foules*, 1895) and Wilfred Trotter (*Instincts of the Herd in Peace and War*, 1916), both of whom referred to the public as the "herd", Bernays writes in *Propaganda*:

Trotter and Le Bon concluded that the group mind does not *think* in the strict sense of the word. In place of thoughts it has impulses, habits, and emotions. In making up its mind, its first impulse is usually to follow the example of a trusted leader. This is one of the most firmly established principles of mass psychology.[30(p73)]

Bernays later changed the word "propaganda" to "public relations" because the former term had acquired a pejorative tone that could not be easily overcome, but the methods remained the same and were applied by him in areas as diverse as consumerism and foreign policy. In his well-known article "Manipulating Public Opinion: The Why and How" (1928), Bernays explains that public opinion can be manipulated in two ways, through propaganda (public relations) and through advertising. In his book *The Father of Spin* (1998), Larry Tye discusses in detail Bernays' promotion of "Lucky Strike" cigarettes and his involvement in the CIA overthrow of the democratically elected government of Guatemala in 1954.

The methods of propaganda developed by Bernays have become classic in the arena of manipulating public opinion and are still being used by politicians of both political parties in the United States. Much of that which is presented to the public by the leading political families in the US comes straight out of the textbook of Edward Bernays. Where the public is held in disdain and manipulated by the techniques of mass psychology, community-building based on communication among individual members of society becomes incredibly difficult. Mass media has exacerbated the situation to the point that the limited communication among citizens which does still take place has been reduced to a parroting of clichés provided by the elite. The result is this: Instead of *our* building *community*, the *elite* (Bernays' "intelligent few") build *consent*. To be sure, a consensus within a community is sometimes necessary, but the experience of community goes much deeper than the manufactured consent of propaganda. Manufactured consent is based primarily — as Bernays makes clear — on a temporary manipulation of the emotions of the public, whereas authentic community-building communication is based on common traditions, shared responsibilities and a deep sense of belonging together. Community-building is a part of culture and must be cultivated. At times, a general consensus on issues may be necessary, but such consensus must be the result of rational thought and critical analysis, not simply an ephemeral expression of emotion. In considering human rights, the granting of certain rights based on manipulated public opinion will inevitably prove to be a divisive factor in society. A superficial acknowledgement of human rights in a particular area cannot stave off a backlash and therefore will never facilitate real community-building. This was one of the weaknesses of the civil rights movement of the twentieth century; far too little attention was given to authentic community-building.

Let us consider now another case in which the opportunity for community-building was offered, but unfortunately missed. The "Universal Declaration of Human Rights" adopted by the United Nations on December 10, 1948 declares in Article 26 that education is a fundamental human right: "Everyone has the right to education. Education shall be free, at least in the elementary and fundamental stages. Elementary education shall be compulsory. Technical and professional education shall be made generally available and higher education shall be equally accessible to all on the basis of merit." In view of this, one might expect that education in an advanced country like the US would have a similar status. Admittedly, education is not explicitly mentioned in the US Constitutional, but the Supreme Court of the United States periodically interprets the Constitution in such a way that a new human right is established. Most recently, same-sex marriage has been ruled a Constitutional right under the "Due Process Clause" and "Equal Protection Clause" of the Fourteenth Amendment, although this Amendment does not mention marriage.

When the right of education was debated in the Supreme Court in 1973 (*San Antonio Independent School District v. Rodriguez*), Justice Powell, who delivered the opinion of the Court, stated that the "Equal Protection Clause" of the Fourteenth Amendment does not apply to the education of children. In dissent, Justice Thurgood Marshall warned that "the majority's holding can only be seen as a retreat from our historic commitment to equality of educational opportunity and as unsupportable acquiescence in a system which deprives children in their earliest years of the chance to reach their full potential as citizens".

Apart from the legal issues involved, one cannot resist posing the question about community-building. Would it not have been community-building to guarantee the right of equal education to every child? Does participation in a democracy not require that every individual be educated to the point of understanding the political system and the issues involved? Would the entire nation not prosper if its citizenry were better educated? Education benefits not only the individual who receives it; the education of each individual benefits the community as a whole. It is significant that Justice Marshall referred to education as a means of developing the "full potential (of children) as citizens". Education is never simply a private matter, and in the interest of community-building, it should be made available to all. A better educated public would be less susceptible to the political propaganda of the mass media und more capable of making moral and political decisions in the interest of all concerned. Since the Court decision in 1973, the quality of American public elementary and secondary education has dropped considerably in comparison with public education in other leading nations.

So far we have discussed three human rights that have been introduced into modern societies: the right of free speech, the right of same-sex marriage and the right of education. Only in passing have we mentioned the right of private property as it is expressed in the Bill of Rights of the United States. We now turn to this topic in more detail in order to illuminate further the guideposts: respectful dialogue, opportuneness of action and community-building. It is important to bear in mind that we are not replacing the concept of human rights, but rather we are providing a context in which to interpret them. Since human rights are the only generally accepted measure for moral and civic conduct in our world, any attempt to disregard them would undoubtedly have disastrous consequences. Therefore, the importance of human rights in the Western world should not be neglected in an attempt to fulfill the requirements of natural law. What we are suggesting is simply this: Human rights should be understood and interpreted in the context of natural law, which strives toward the common good.

As we have noted several times, there was a shift in emphasis on human rights from the time of the US Declaration of Independence to the drafting of the US Constitution. In spite of what many Americans believe, the Founders never intended for the United States to be a democracy, and consequently, they established it from the beginning as a Republic, adopting certain ideas about human rights and property from the English philosopher John Locke. The phrase "Life, Liberty and the

Pursuit of Happiness" in the Declaration of Independence served well to inspire the colonists to revolution, but when the Bill of Rights was added to the Constitution, the Founders abandoned this phrase in favor of the right to "Life, Liberty and *Property*". The introduction of the concept of property at this point gave Amendment V a strong Lockean tone that has remained a part of the American mentality. In 1703, John Locke himself commented: "Property I have nowhere found more clearly explained, than in a book entitled, Two Treatises of Government."[31(p3)] Odd as it may seem that Locke referred to his own book in this way, he was certainly correct in viewing his understanding of property as groundbreaking in political philosophy. From the time that his *Two Treatises of Government* appeared in 1690, readers have been surprised by the way in which he founded political society on the concept of private property.

At the beginning of *The Second Treatise of Government*, Locke describes the state of nature before the establishment of political society; it is a state of perfect freedom and equality among all human beings. Furthermore, in the original state of nature, the entire world belonged to humankind in common, and therefore private property was excluded.

God, who hath given the World to Men in common, hath also given them reason to make use of it to the best advantage of Life, and convenience. The Earth, and all that is therein, is given to Men for the Support and Comfort of their being. And though all the Fruits it naturally produces, and Beasts it feeds, belong to Mankind in common, as they are produced by the spontaneous hand of Nature; and no body has originally a private Dominion, exclusive of the rest of Mankind, in any of them, as they are thus in their natural state: yet being given for the use of Men, there must of necessity be a means *to appropriate* them some way or other before they can be of any use, or at all beneficial to any particular Man.[31(2.26)]

Both philosophically and religiously, Locke felt that he was on solid ground in describing the state of nature as one in which all things were held in common, but the transition from an original communism to private property presented him with a challenge. His solution to this problem was to establish the principle that each individual has a property in his or her own person, and consequently, the labor performed by the person is also a possession. Locke writes:

> Though the Earth, and all inferior Creatures be common to all Men, yet every Man has a *Property* in his own *Person*. This no Body has any Right to but himself. The *Labour* of his Body, and the *Work* of his Hands, we may say, are properly his. Whatsoever then he removes out of the State that Nature hath provided, and left it in, he hath mixed his *Labour* with, and joyned to it something that is his own, and thereby makes it his *Property*. It being by him removed from the common state Nature placed it in, it hath by this *labour* something annexed to it, that excludes the common right of other Men.[31(2.27)]

In this short section, Locke postulates a libertarian view of the body—the person *owns* his or her own body—and justifies private property by means of the body's labor. Just as the *body* is the property of the individual, the *labor* of the body is also the property of the individual, and when this labor is attached to anything in the common state of nature, that thing becomes the property of the individual as well.

So the labor exerted in the process of making a part of nature useable provides the transition from communism to private property. This does not mean, however, that an individual has the right to accumulate as much as possible of the natural resources of the earth. Locke writes: "As much as any one can make use of to any advantage of life before it spoils; beyond this, is more than his share, and belongs to others."[31(2.31)] In specifying a limit to the acquisition of private property, Locke emphasizes that the property must be used before it spoils. In reading Locke's *The Second Treatise of Government*, it is clear that he assumes a boundless supply of natural resources. If each person only appropriates that which can be used before it spoils, then there will be an ample supply for everyone. Even in the case of land, Locke thought that there was enough for everyone, if each person only claimed as much as he could till and cultivate. As he stated the matter: "No Body could think himself injur'd by the drinking of another Man, though he took a good Draught, who had a whole River of the same Water left him to quench his thirst. And the Case of Land and Water, where there is enough of both, is perfectly the same."[31(2.35)]

Had Locke's analysis of private property concluded at this point, it would have been in many ways more equitable, but having established the right of private property, he introduces the use of money, which is not perishable und can therefore be accumulated without spoilage. Whereas the accumulation of property was originally limited by the condition of labor and actual usage, "the *Invention of money*, and the tacit Agreement of Men to put a value on it, introduced (by Consent) larger Possessions, and a Right to them..."[31(2.36)] That is, after the introduction of money in the form of gold and silver, a person had a right, according to Locke, to "heap up as much of these durable things as he pleased"[31(2.46)] and by so doing, the person would not infringe in any way on the rights of others.

After he has established that the right of private property is grounded in the proprietorship of one's body and that it is anterior to the formation of any government, Locke proceeds to claim that governments were established for the expressed purpose of protecting private property.

And 'tis not without reason, that he [man in the original state of nature] seeks out, and is willing to joyn in Society with others who are already united, or have a mind to unite for the mutual *Preservation* of their Lives, Liberties and Estates, which I call by the general Name, *Property*. The great and *chief end* therefore, of Mens uniting into Commonwealths, and putting themselves under Government, *is the Preservation of their Property*.[31](2.123f)

It cannot be emphasized too much that the United States has been profoundly affected by John Locke's understanding of property and government. Following the American Revolution, the ideas of Locke's *Second Treatise of Government* were mediated to the United States to a great extent through the *Commentaries on the Laws of England* by Sir William Blackstone, the renowned English jurist whose understanding of property rights was even more radical than Locke's.[29(p22–25)] According to Blackstone, property rights are absolute and exclusive. Since Blackstone's primary focus was on property rights, those aspects of Locke's *Second Treatise of Government* that stress the duty and responsibility of citizens tended to be overshadowed. Thus it happened that the fledgling New World adopted an understanding of property rights that was—especially in comparison with Continental Europe—very one-sided. Especially on an emotional level, property rights are viewed in the US as individual, absolute and exclusive. However, this is not the last word on the matter.

Even if Americans tend to *feel* that their property rights are absolute, they *know* from experience that there are limitations placed on these rights; that is, property rights are not really absolute. Take the fictitious case of Mr Smith who owns a small farm inside the city limits of a growing community. If the city decides to expand and build a new residential area beyond Smith's farm, the City Council will undoubtedly approach Smith about an easement across his property for the necessary water and wastewater facilities. Should Mr Smith refuse to allow access to his property on the grounds that his property rights are absolute, the case may indeed come before a judge where, in all likelihood, the common good of the community will take precedence over the property rights of Mr Smith. If we were to consider an actual case of this sort, we would find that a successful outcome of the conflicting claims of the individual and the city involved in some way the application of the guideposts: respectful dialogue, opportuneness of action and community-building.

Although most people would consider the previous case of an easement to be rather straightforward, opinions vary widely on the matter of taxation for the well-being of the entire citizenry of the nation. Especially those individuals who have accumulated enormous wealth in the libertarian style of Locke tend to view taxation for the benefit of the commonwealth as an infringement on their property rights. However, if such property rights are not absolute, they must be placed within the context of the common good. That is, we must follow the guideposts for the common good in assessing the legitimacy of these rights in particular situations.

The guidepost "respectful dialogue" requires that the wealthiest members of society engage in conversation with all other social and economic strata including the neediest citizens of the country. Publications sponsored by conservative groups such as "Americans for Prosperity" do not constitute dialogue; authentic dialogue requires personal contact between individuals who represent opposing or contrasting views. Furthermore, the dynamic of conversation can only take place when each party makes an honest attempt to understand and to empathize with the position of the other. Such respectful dialogue between the wealthiest and the neediest of society would have to overcome many technical difficulties and would necessarily proceed in stages involving different levels of society. But in the end, the real obstacle to such respectful dialogue is not technical, but rather emotional. It would require a considerable measure of good will on the part of the individuals involved and would be fraught with moments of awkwardness and unpleasantness. Still, it should be remembered: The life of excellence is not easily attained.

The second guidepost, the "opportuneness of events", would direct our attention once again to the libertarian doctrine of John Locke in *The Second Treatise of Government* in order to evaluate its appropriateness in today's world. As we have seen, Locke did not think that the accumulation of wealth in the form of imperishable money would infringe on the rights of other members of society. It is, however, important to note that Locke's doctrine of economics and politics is based on a fable about the original situation of human beings before the establishment of any society and that this fable does not correspond to any known historical society. Accepting uncritically the libertarian views of Locke on economics is as nonsensical as patterning one's marriage relationship on Adam and Eve. To be sure, Locke's fable is not without merit, but it must be viewed critically. First of all, he assumes a population of individuals much smaller than we have at present; since 1700, the world population has increased by a factor of ten. Secondly, he assumes a world of unlimited resources, which is at best unrealistic. Thirdly, he assumes that each and every individual has the physical and mental capacity to labor and to acquire private property. In his fable, there are no handicapped individuals; there are no mentally retarded persons; there are no individuals plagued by anxiety and depression. Locke's world resembles the game of Monopoly more than it does the actual world; in his fable, everyone starts the game with an equal chance of success. This is not, however, the world in which actual human beings live. In the real world, there are privileged individuals from affluent families who attend Ivy League schools, and there are poverty stricken individuals who cannot rise above the depression of a slum. Faced with the realities of an unfair and imperfect world, the question inevitably arises: How is the accumulation of wealth to be understood in this situation? Since property rights are not absolute, the taxation of this wealth would seem justified in order to ensure the human dignity of each and every citizen.

"Community-building", our third guidepost, reminds us that we are in fact members of a community, and this judgment applies to the wealthiest as well as to the poorest citizens of society. The attempt of the financial elite of society to separate themselves from "ordinary" citizens is not only morally despicable, it is philosophically ludicrous. The notion of the "self-made" man who is independent and self-sufficient is, in a word, foolish. We inherit a tradition that was forged by others over centuries. We live in a culture that we did not create. We speak a language that we received as a gift from others. And the very language that we speak binds us together with other citizens, past and present. We benefit today from the labors of our predecessors who built a community, nourished a culture and transmitted a language, and as recipients of these benefits, we bear the responsibility of community-building in our time and in our part of the world. Some have argued that the increased taxation of the wealthy would lead to unemployment and to a general deterioration of society. Such claims should be scrutinized carefully. Others have argued that increased taxation is absolutely necessary for community-building and that it has only been resisted by the wealthy because of their greed. These claims too must be scrutinized. If we are truly committed to community-building, unfounded claims about the effects of taxation cannot be accepted. Central to the analysis of all claims must be the twofold realization that property rights are not absolute and that community-building is an essential part of human nature.

At the end of our search for the common good, it cannot be claimed that we have reached our goal. The atrocities of National

Socialism in Germany during the 1930s and 1940s remain in our historical consciousness as a warning against identifying the common good with the interests of the State. At the same time, the extremely limited focus on the concept of human rights since the 1960s has proven to be inadequate as a basis for responsible moral and political decisions. For this reason, we have maintained in the present work that human rights should always be viewed against the background of the common good, and we have made the attempt to sketch out an understanding of the common good that avoids some of the pitfalls of the past. Since we live today in a very pluralistic society, we have considered the Judeo-Christian tradition only to the extent that it has been historically significant, and in the interest of neutrality, we have taken our starting point from the pre-Christian classical writings of Cicero. In particular, we have provided a modern interpretation of Cicero's notion of natural law through an analysis of the self and its place in society. In the final chapter, we arrived at three guideposts for moral reflection: respectful dialogue, opportuneness of action and community-building. The word "guidepost" was carefully chosen in order to indicate the undogmatic character of our conclusions. These guideposts are not rules, but simply indicators. Likewise, our entire presentation is not to be understood as a rigid system, but rather as an invitation to enter into a process that will hopefully enable us to restore the moral dimension of society and the moral authority of the nation. The eclipse of moral authority, which we described in Chapter 1, will not be remedied as long as the hostility of opposing parties dominates the national scene. The desperate clinging to external standards—whether these are of a religious or philosophical nature is irrelevant—has resulted in a divisiveness that can only be overcome by mutual participation in a process focusing on dialogue and compromise. Formulating ideas and writing essays are relatively easy endeavors; living through the process together will be considerably more difficult.

References

1. Brush J. *Glauben als Ereignis: Selbst, Kraft, Zeit, Leben*. Berlin, Germany: LIT Verlag; 2011.
2. Harrelson W. Law in the OT. *The Interpreter's Dictionary of the Bible*, vol. 3. New York: Abingdon Press; 1962. p. 77–89.
3. Zilsel E. *Die sozialen Ursprünge der neuzeitlichen Wissenschaft*. Frankfurt am Main: Suhrkamp Verlag; 1976.
4. Robinson J. *An Introduction to Early Greek Philosophy*. Boston: Houghton Mifflin Company; 1968.
5. Hampe M. *Eine kleine Geschichte des Naturgesetzbegriffs*. Frankfurt am Main: Suhrkamp Verlag; 2007.
6. Long A, Sedley D. *The Hellenistic Philosophers, vol. 1.* Cambridge: Cambridge University Press; 1987.
7. Cicero. "On the Laws". in: *On the Commonwealth and On the Laws*. ed. James Zetzel. Cambridge: Cambridge University Press; 1999. p. 105–175.
8. Cicero. "On the Commonwealth". in: *On the Commonwealth and On the Laws*. ed. James Zetzel. Cambridge: Cambridge University Press; 1999. p. 1–103.
9. Cicero. *On Duties*. ed. M. T. Griffin, E. M. Atkins. Cambridge: Cambridge University Press; 1991.
10. Cicero. *On the Ends of Good and Evil*. transl. H. Rackham. Cambridge, MA: Harvard University Press; 1983.
11. Bacon F. *The New Organon or True Directions Concerning the Interpretation of Nature* (1620). In: The Works, vol. 8. ed. J. Spedding, R. L. Ellis and D. D. Heath. Boston: Taggard and Thompson; 1863.
12. Descartes R. *Principia Philosophiae* (1644). Hamburg: Felix Meiner Verlag; 2005.
13. Newton I. *Principia Mathematica, Opera, vol. 2 & 3*. ed. Samuel Horsley, 1782.
14. Newton I. *Opticks*. Query 31 (2nd ed. 1717). Opera, vol. 4; 1988.

15. Darwin C. *Descent of Man. vol. 1.* London: John Murray; 1871.

16. Rickman H. *Pattern and Meaning in History.* New York: Harper & Row, Publishers; 1962.

17. Hahn H. *The Old Testament in Modern Research.* Philadelphia: Fortress Press; 1966.

18. Pritchard J. *Ancient Near Eastern Texts.* Princeton: Princeton University Press; 1955.

19. Cohen-Tannoudji G. *Universal Constants in Physics.* New York: McGraw-Hill; 1993.

20. Jammer M. *Concepts of Force* (1957). Mineola, New York: Dover Publications, Inc.; 1999.

21. Paley W. *Natural Theology or Evidence of the Existence and Attributes of the Deity, collected from the appearances of nature* (1802). Oxford: Oxford University Press; 2008.

22. Michelson A. *Light Waves and Their Uses* (1903). Chicago: University of Chicago Press; 1907.

23. Plato. *Timaios.* 37d5.

24. Castells M. *The Rise of the Network Society.* United Kingdom: Wiley-Blackwell; 2010.

25. Rogers C. *On Becoming a Person.* Boston: Houghton Mifflin Company; 1961.

26. Fischer D. *Albion's Seed: Four British Folkways in America.* New York: Oxford University Press; 1989.

27. Zetzel J. "Introduction". in: Cicero: *On the Commonwealth and On the Laws.* Cambridge: Cambridge University Press; 1999.

28. Hobbes T. *Leviathan.* Cambridge: Cambridge University Press; 1996.

29. Glendon M. *Rights Talk: The Impoverishment of Political Discourse.* New York: The Free Press; 1991.

30. Bernays E. *Propaganda.* New York: Ig Publishing; 1928.

31. Locke J. *Two Treatises of Government* (1690). ed. Peter Laslett. Cambridge: Cambridge University Press; 1988.

BOOKS

Iff Books is interested in ideas and reasoning. It publishes material on science, philosophy and law. Iff Books aims to work with authors and titles that augment our understanding of the human condition, society and civilisation, and the world or universe in which we live.